THE
BOOK
OF
Revelation

THE
BOOK
OF
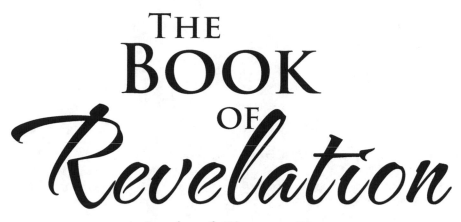
Revelation

A Study of Christ in You,
the Hope of Glory

(Vol. 2) Chapters 8-13

BISHOP AUDREY DRUMMONDS, PH.D.

authorHOUSE®

AuthorHouse™
1663 Liberty Drive
Bloomington, IN 47403
www.authorhouse.com
Phone: 833-262-8899

Published by AuthorHouse 09/29/2021

ISBN: 978-1-5049-8122-4 (sc)
ISBN: 978-1-5049-8121-7 (e)

Print information available on the last page.

Any people depicted in stock imagery provided by Thinkstock are models, and such images are being used for illustrative purposes only. Certain stock imagery © Thinkstock.

This book is printed on acid-free paper.

Table of Contents

Preface xi

Author's Notes..xvii

Introduction..xix

Chapter 8: Silence in Heaven, and then…....................................1

Chapter 9: Final Trumpet Sounds..25

Chapter 10: A Strong Angel..64

Chapter 11: The Two Prophets of God...89

Chapter 12: The Woman Gives Birth to a Son..........................127

Chapter 13: The Beast 173

Scripture References..209

Appendix: Our Identity in Christ Today....................................215

Reading Resources 217

About the author 221

Preface

In Matthew 6:9-13, Jesus showed the world how to pray:

"Our Father in heaven,
hallowed be your name,
your kingdom come,
your will be done
on earth as it is in heaven.
Give us today our daily bread.
Forgive us our debts,
as we also have forgiven our debtors.
And lead us not into temptation,
but deliver us from the evil one." (NIV)

*M*any of us have memorized these verses yet never stopped to consider what the words "our Father" signifies to who we are. What is the root level of our identity to call God Father? Jesus taught humanity to address the Almighty God as "Father." This was before Jesus went to Calvary or resurrected from the grave! The people Jesus taught this prayer to would have understood that by addressing someone as "father" would be a public declaration of a birthright to being that person's son or daughter, and heir to their possessions and family authority. Declaring God as their "Father" was the highest order of blasphemy known to the Jewish people and subject to the penalty of death. If anyone were caught praying this prayer, a prayer most people today don't even give reverence to when voiced, they would have been declared dead by the High Priest. It was his job to be the intercessor for the people through the blood of the animal sacrifices. However, declaring God as "Father" was a sin that the High Priest would not have been able to intervene for the people. This was blasphemy on the highest level. According to the Jewish law, if one person uttered this prayer, it had the power of such great magnitude to cause separation and death from God upon the entire nation.

As powerful as the words of this prayer are, it was the prayer of the people of God, not the "Lord's prayer." The prayer that Lord Jesus prayed to God His Father can be found in John 17:

> *"These things Jesus spake, and when he had cast up his eyes into heaven [and the eyes lifted up to heaven], he said, Father, the hour cometh, clarify thy Son, that thy Son clarify thee. As thou hast given to him power on each flesh, that all thing that thou hast given to him, he give to them everlasting life. And this is everlasting life, that they know thee very God alone [that they know thee alone very God], and whom thou hast sent, Jesus Christ. I have clarified thee on the earth;* **I have ended the work that thou hast given to me to do. And now, Father, clarify thou me at thyself, with the clearness that I had at thee, before the world was made.** *I have showed thy name to those men, which thou hast given to me of the world [I have showed thy name to the men, whom thou hast given to me of the world]; they were thine, and thou hast given them to me, and they have kept thy word. And now they have known, that all things that thou hast given to me, be of thee. For the words that thou hast given to me, I gave to them; and they have taken, and have known verily, that I went out from thee; and they believed, that thou sentest me. I pray for them, I pray not for the world, but for them that thou hast given to me, for they be thine. And*

*all my things be thine, and thy things be mine [And all mine things be thine, and thine things be mine]; and I am clarified in them. And now I am not in the world, and these be in the world, and I come to thee. Holy Father, keep them in thy name, which thou hast given to me [whom thou hast given to me], that they be one, as we be. While I was with them, I kept them in thy name; those that thou gavest to me, I kept, and none of them perished, but the son of perdition, that the scripture be fulfilled. But now I come to thee, and I speak these things in the world [and these things I speak in the world], that they have my joy fulfilled in themselves. I gave to them thy word, and the world had them in hate; for they be not of the world, as I am not of the world. I pray not, that thou take them away from the world, but that thou keep them from evil. They be not of the world, as I am not of the world. Hallow thou them in truth; thy word is truth. As thou sentest me into the world, also I sent them into the world. And I hallow myself for them, that also they be hallowed in truth. **And I pray not only for them, but also for them that shall believe into me by the word of them; that all be one [that all they be one], as thou, Father, in me, and I in thee, that also they in us be one; that the world believe, that thou hast sent me.** And I have given to them the clearness, that thou hast given to me, that they be one, as we be one; I in them, and thou in me, that they be ended into one; and that the world know, that thou sentest me, and hast loved them, as thou hast loved also me. Father, they which thou hast given to me, I will that where I am, that they be with me, that they see my clearness, that thou hast given to me [Father, I will that and they whom thou hast given to me, be with me where I am, that they see my clearness, which thou hast given to me]; for thou lovedest me before the making of the world. Father, rightfully the world knew thee not [Rightful Father, the world knew not* *thee], but I knew thee, and these knew, that thou sentest me. And I have made thy name known to them, and shall make known; that the love by which thou hast loved me, be in them, and I in them."*

The difference between what Jesus taught the disciples to pray and what He prayed himself was the difference in the heart of knowing God as His child or knowing God by being His son and doing the family's business by bringing unity to the body of Christ as one body.

The Gospel of John teaches us that we are the children of God. When we move on to the Epistles of John, we learn that the children of God are transforming into sons of God. This is where most Christian stop in their growth and development of their identity in Christ. **For those that have been called to search the book of Revelation, John let's us know in the beginning of this book that it is for the kings and priests on the earth today (Rev. 1:6)** that know the Most High God as Father, and they are called to rule and reign with Jesus Christ from heavenly places. *"In this [union and communion with Him] love is brought to completion and attains perfection with us, that we may have confidence for the day of judgment [with assurance and boldness to face Him], because as He is, so are we in this world.* (1 John 4:17, Amplified Bible).

Judgment day was satisfied at Calvary where the death of Jesus was my death and the resurrection of Christ was my resurrection. *"I have been crucified with Christ and I no longer live, but Christ lives in me. The life I live in the body, I live by faith in the Son of God, who loved me and gave himself for me"* (Gal. 2:20, NIV).

In 2 Corinthians 5:16-21 Paul tells us, *"Therefore we from this time know no man after the flesh; though we (have) known Christ after the flesh [And so we from this time have known no man after the flesh; and if we knew Christ after the flesh], but [right] now we know not. Therefore if any new creature is in Christ, the old things be passed [old things have passed]*. **Lo! All things be made new, and all things be of God, which reconciled us to him by Christ, and gave to us the service of reconciling [and gave to us the ministry, or service, of reconciling]. And God was in Christ** *[Soothly, for God was in Christ], reconciling to him the world, not reckoning to them their guilt, and putted in us the word of reconciling [and put in us the word of reconciling]. Therefore we use message for Christ [Therefore we be set in legacy, or message, for Christ], as if God admonisheth by us; we beseech you for Christ, be ye reconciled to God. God the Father made him sin for us, which knew not sin, that we should be made [the] righteousness of God in him"* (WYC).

If the book of Revelation is read from a mindset that is anything less than the "mind of Christ" (1 Cor. 2:16), there is danger to the body of Christ. It would be likened to giving a five-year old the keys to a semi-truck and allowing him to drive it going 100 miles an hour on a busy interstate; or handing a three-year old a box of matches and telling him to make a fire and cook a meal over an open camp fire. Many of the books and commentaries that are available on the book of Revelation have taken an approach of doom and gloom. This has caused the body of Christ to be so full of fear of "end times" that their focus has been on saving themselves from the "great tribulation" instead of realizing that **THE BODY OF CHRIST involves uniting ALL of humanity, which is why** *"the body of Jesus Christ died once for ALL"* (Heb. 10:10)!

When we come to the next book, we will find in Revelation 14:6 another angel having the **"everlasting gospel to preach to them that dwell on the earth. What is this gospel?** It is the death, burial, and resurrection of Jesus Christ, the first-born raised from the dead, and the first fruits of those that slept. It is by man that death came and it is by man that there is the resurrection of the dead that in Christ all will be made alive (1 Corinthians 15).

In Isaiah chapter eleven, God tells us how to understand His ways. We must begin by obtaining the Spirit of Wisdom. The secrets of

God can only be given to those He chooses by His sovereign grace, to not only take others to the steps of His Holy Temple, but to bring them into His Holy presence.

If your heart yearns to enter into His gates and be transformed into His image... for His glory, desiring to bring unity to the body of Christ; then turn the pages of this book. However; be warned, for there will be the destruction of "self, religion, and ego" as you go through transfiguration into your call and position to rule and reign with the KING of kings and LORD of lords...

Author's Notes

*A*s a little girl, I would go with my family to different country churches where my father would be the guest pastor. As we would travel to our destination, many thoughts of a five year old would be going off in my head. Should I be nervous and scared meeting all the many new faces; would I be able to sit still and not draw attention while my father preached; could I keep my frilly Sunday dress clean; could I stay awake during the service? So many concerns for a little one surrounding the one desire simply to please my parents.

I knew that a lot of my discomfort would be resolved if my father was preaching on something that would keep the interest of a child.

"Mommy, what is daddy going to talk to the people about today in church?" I would ask. Since my father did not have to prepare a new sermon each week for the same congregation, he would often teach from a selection that he was already familiar with and could present with ease allowing the wisdom of God to flow from his words with elegance and power.

"Your father is going to preach today about when God asked Ezekiel if the bones can live" (Ezekiel 37:3).This was my favorite teaching to hear and instantly my mother's words caused all my anxieties to diminish.

With a child like imagination, I would visualize a massive field full of skeletons scattered over a hot, sandy desert with no water in sight. As my father would preach from Ezekiel 37, I would see the skeletons responding to the word of the Lord: The foot bones connecting to the ankle bones, and the ankle bones connecting to the leg bones, the leg bones connecting to the hip bones, etc. till all the bones were connected. Then I would visualize skin and hair and faces created from the skeletons that were formed. Finally, I would wait with anticipation of a great wind blowing across this dry land and life would enter into the people that were once dead but had now become the great army of God's love and mercy.

Whenever my dad would preach, I would sit on the front row of the church with my mother and brothers. Little did I know that it was the voice of my Heavenly Father speaking to me through my natural father saying, *"prophesy upon these bones, and say unto them, O ye dry bones, hear the word of the Lord…Behold, I will cause breath to enter into you, and ye shall live"* (Ezekiel 37:4-5).

Fifty years later, I prophesied as my Heavenly Father commanded me…

Jesus Christ was the only man alive at the time of his natural birth. Since His death and resurrection over 2000 years ago, there have been no more dead men…

Thank you dad for training me up in the way God wanted me to go. Thank you for being a vessel He was able to speak through.

Introduction

*T*he Apostle John wrote the Book of Revelation. What he wrote is the revelation of Jesus Christ, not revelations. There have been several views of how this book can be interpreted. Each view has its own interpretation. The author has chosen to interpret it from the "finished work of Jesus Christ" that was declared in John 19:30. This book is viewed in unity with all the books of the Bible as the mind of God; and can only be understood with spiritual understanding. The interpretation is with the belief that there is an unveiling of our true identity in Christ revealed to each of us only by the Holy Spirit. The eternal wisdom that God has for the body of Christ cannot be contained in one individual's understanding. It takes the unity of the whole body for the Lord's return to be manifested.

The word "revelation" is singular, not plural. This is a key to understanding these Scriptures. God gave the writing to John to disclose **the unveiling of the divine mysteries throughout Scripture** (Ephesians 3:14-17). The author does not say this is a book about demonic power, terrorism, or eternal hell; nor is it about beastly creatures, Iraq, scud-missiles, or monsters. Revelation was not written to scare people into Christianity, but to bless them if they read it – to have within the believer the dunamis power of God called GRACE to witness resurrection life in the walking dead of mankind.

Acts 4:33 tells us when revelation knowledge is given; the unveiling of that revelation will bring forth great grace, loving-kindness,

favor, and goodwill. John writes in Revelation 1:3 that you will be blessed, happy, and envied by reading, hearing, and keeping yourself true to the things that are written. He does not say you will be scared, beaten, judged, or condemned; but blessed to be envied. This is so that others will be drawn to the same revelation of Jesus Christ through His love and mercy that they see in your life.

This is the only book in the Bible that tells us what the book is about in the first verse. However, for us to understand the book we must already know in our spirit that we have "ears to hear" what the Spirit of God says. If every verse had to be qualified for understanding, it would be a process of dissecting the entire Bible to understand the one verse.

This book is an unveiling of Jesus Christ, THE WORD. It is known as the Apocalypse of the New Testament, which means to uncover something that is hidden. It has been there ALL through time, but the veiling of our natural understanding did not allow us to see it.

There was no veil within the temple of God after Calvary. It was torn from top to bottom when Jesus hung on the cross (Luke 23:45). The veil we have to deal with today is our mind, which has allowed religion to separate us from the ability to be in the Holy of Holies. Jesus told us over 2000 years ago that the work is finished; the Messiah has come (John 19:30). Religion tells us that it is not finished; we still have to deal with the body of Jesus (John 19:31). Today, religion is still trying to make sure the body of Jesus is dead (John 19:31), when according to the Apostle Paul we died (Galatians 2:20). Selah.

The primary work of the Holy Spirit when studying this book will be to remove the veil called the "hanging" that separated the middle and inner courts of the temple of God in the Old Testament. This veil is symbolic of Jesus Christ hanging on the cross. Today, it is our hanging, or our imagination, represented by cherubim that must be pulled back. **This book reveals how we, as priests, are to be transformed into His image as High Priest.** This is not a book about the saved and unsaved people on this earth, or who is escaping to heaven and who will be tormented in hell. As the Holy Spirit brings forth spiritual understanding we must come to the cross and hang our natural understanding allowing the Life of Christ in us to be resurrected and manifested through us.

Have you ever wondered, among all the followers of Jesus, why John was chosen to write the Book of Revelation? Several times, in chapters two and three, John wrote that you must have "an ear to hear." He did not write this to non-Christians, but to those who were believers in Christ. This book is about Jesus (the door). John was the one who had his ear nailed to the door by leaning on the breast of Jesus and hearing his heart (John 13:23, 21:20).

It takes a bondservant that is willing to have his ear pierced to the door to have an ear to hear what the Spirit of God is revealing. **A bondservant is a person who gives their life to serve Jesus Christ and ALL whom Jesus calls the family of God, not just those the church views as family.**

In Chapter 1 verse one, we read the words, "which must shortly come to pass." This is not only a futurist book, but also a book that shows us past, present, and future (Eccl. 3:15, Isaiah 46:10). The Alpha and the Omega, in verse 8 of this chapter, tells us; what has come, what will come, and what is now. **The word NOW is an eternal word for it has no time.** Understanding the revelation of Jesus Christ takes the future and the past and brings it into the now. The

John knew when he wrote this book that Jesus died for the sins of the world allowing the Holy Spirit to draw ALL men to God so that God would be ALL in all.

time is at hand (verse 1:3) is your hand. For some people, this book will stay in the content of shortly happening, but for others that seek out for the veil to be removed completely, the time will be NOW.

In this same verse, we see the word "signified" which can be found in Strong's Concordance to mean, "To give a sign, to express by signs and symbols." John tells us it is written in code. The rule of Hermeneutics taught in Bible schools, is that if you are going to interpret a set of scriptures you must stay consistent with your principles. If you started with literal interpretations then you must stay literal. If you interpret scripture spiritually, then you must continue with spiritual. You cannot switch back and forth or the interpretations are disqualified. An illustration would be the interpretation of the "Lamb slain" in the Book of Revelation. It is usually accepted that John was talking about Jesus Christ, and not a literal lamb.

Another example would be in Revelation 2:16 that says, "With the sword of my mouth." Most churches across America have no problem with this being symbolism of the word of God being spoken with power and authority, not a literal sword coming out of the mouth of Jesus.

The frustration in understanding the Book of Revelation comes when teachers do not continue with the same principle. Instead, they select which symbols they want to be spiritual and which they want to be literal. If the lamb is a symbol then we need to see the temple, the beast, the candlestick, etc. with the same Hermeneutical Principle, and not a building, a creature, or a tabletop decoration. John tells us in the beginning that he was in the spirit when these things were revealed to him. The things of the Spirit of God will seem to be foolishness to the mind of the natural man (1 Corinthians 1:25). John was given spiritual truth about Jesus Christ using signs and symbols, and he clarified this in the first chapter. The rest of the book should also be interpreted with spiritual symbolism to stay consistent with this principle.

When Jesus talked with religious leaders, he used this same principle. He would use spiritual illustrations; unfortunately, they would apply literal meaning causing misunderstanding with what Jesus was saying. For example: The illustration of the temple being destroyed and Jesus rebuilding it in 3 days (John 2:19-21). They were looking at His words from an Old Covenant mindset, and He was speaking New Covenant. It was not only what Jesus said that upset the religious leaders, but what they thought he said. Jesus used events and ways of life in their culture to illustrate how the Old Testament Scriptures and concepts are to be interpreted in the NOW. The types and shadows of literal understanding given to us in the Old Testament have been unveiled into a present Now with the revelation of Jesus Christ.

I would like to reemphasize that the Book of Revelation is about Jesus Christ (period). It is not about Jesus, plus something else. The mystery that is revealed to John as he sees Jesus, the Alpha and Omega, is not to see a man, but to see Jesus who is the head, to be attached to the church, which is his body. **We should be looking for His appearing in His body – you and me, which has many facets of color and radiance reflecting His glory. We must decide if Jesus died and rose from the grave for our spirit now and our soul and body later; or if we possess the fullness of whom He is today?** If we believe a little now, and the rest when we get to heaven, we will not see the return of Jesus while in our natural body. Selah.

The word "revelation" means the disclosure of truth concerning things before known. This book was in existence before we knew of John's writings. God wrote it in our hearts before the foundation of the world, before Genesis 1:1. God gave us this book, but the understanding was concealed in the language of the Holy Spirit. Our minds became veiled when Adam became his own god instead of keeping unity with the family of God. When he ate the seed of his own words, he separated himself from the throne of God or the mercy seat. He was taken out of the inner court (garden) so that he would not be in a state of judgment and condemnation forever.

God knew that His love would draw ALL men back to Him. *"For there is one God, and one mediator between God and men, the man Christ Jesus"* (1 Timothy 2: 4-5.) He kept a way open with a flaming sword, the Holy Spirit, guarded by Cherubim, or the natural mind of man. The Way is the Lamb, the Son of God, who was slain before the foundation of the world, but we could not understand any of this because it was not time. God wrote this book in our hearts a long time ago, and to each person He gave a time and season for both natural and spiritual growth to take place so that we would be united as one body in Jesus Christ. When God brings understanding to us in the Spirit we are not necessarily supposed to go out and try to convince everyone else. It is the responsibility of the Holy Spirit to be the teacher in each of us, so that God will be glorified and not us. Our job is to utilize our spiritual understanding to be a bondservant for Jesus Christ by seeing ALL men through His eyes that reflect unconditional love and forgiveness from the mercy seat of God. It is in our inner most being where His Spirit communicates with our spirit, not our natural mind.

When we see each member of the body of Christ as complete in Him, the Spirit of God will bring the finished work of Jesus Christ concealed in our heavenly mind into our natural life. God's word is not a game of chance. If our belief system is rooted in God's intended spiritual imagery, then life will result. Where we are rooted and receiving our nourishment from will determine how we grow, and whether we can boldly come to the

> *What we see in our minds as truth forms our believing for "as a man thinks in his heart, so is he" (Proverbs 23:7).*

throne of God while alive in our natural body. We know that God can cure headaches, cancer, major illnesses, etc., but can we dare to believe that it is possible for us to live eternally like Enoch and Elijah not dying a physical death?

Do you see the return of Jesus Christ now, or someday? Are you really looking for His return with spiritual eyes, or carnal understanding? Are you seeing a body that Jesus can place His head on? Religion still tries to destroy the temple of God, (spirit, soul, and body), but Jesus raised it up in three days finishing it all where we are now completed in Him at His resurrection. Today, it is up to us to put all things under His feet (1 Corinthians 15: 25-28).

Think about this - God stood in front of the religious leaders and they did not recognize Him. They thought they were crucifying a man. Would we recognize Him? If you are reading this, then I can say that He has already stood before you, probably many times. How many times is Christ still being crucified with the power of our words?

> *The fruit that grew on the Tree of Life and the Tree of Knowledge of Good and Evil was not an apple, orange, or pear. They were words that had power to create LIFE or death depending on which tree one ate from. (Proverbs 18:21)*

Those that want to be blessed in reading this book need to have their hearts prepared to cross over into the spirit realm while in their natural body. They are people that believe Galatians 2:20 and Ephesians 1:4 with their body, soul, and spirit. They desire an intimate relationship with the Lord, and they are willing to go beyond the boundaries of doctrine and religion to obtain it. They must be prepared for separation and division with the people they are close to, even loved ones if they are not pulled into the same calling that God has placed in them. The people that will be blessed from this book will be going through many trials, yet still have a voice praising God saying, "I surrender ALL, so that I may know you and the power of your resurrection while in my natural body, for it is in You that I live, and move, and am one in Christ Jesus."

I close this introduction with a devotional writing found in a book called, *God Calling* by A.J. Russell. On May 14th we read a message titled "The Love of a Lover:"

Remember that a loving Master delights in the intimacy of demands made, as much as He desires His followers and friends to delight in the tender intimacy of His demands. The wonder of family life is expressed in the freedom with which a child makes demands and claims, quite as much as in the loving demands the parent makes upon all the Love and Joy of the children. Only as the result of frequent converse with Me, of much prayer to Me, of listening to and obedience to My behests comes that intimacy that makes My followers dare to approach Me as friend to friend.

I pray this introduction will challenge you to want to continue to study Revelation into Chapter 8-13 allowing the Holy Spirit to bring Life, Love, and Light of blessings into your NOW. When we come to the next book, we will find in Revelation 14:6 another angel having the "everlasting gospel to preach to them that dwell on the earth. What is this gospel? It is the death, burial, and resurrection of Jesus Christ who is the first-born risen from the dead and the first fruits of those

Almighty God used a woman to bring God into the natural realm where mankind was in bondage. He will use a woman, the church, His bride and wife to redeem the body of Christ.

that slept. It is by man that death came and it is by man that there is the resurrection of the dead that in Christ all will be made alive (1 Corinthians 15).

Jesus said, *"I am not sent but unto the lost sheep of the house of Israel."* (Matthew 15:24). This is a missing link in interpreting John's writings. The questions we must ask is, "Who is Israel?" "Who was given the birthright and who was given the blessings through time that God promised to Abraham's seed?"

These questions are keys to unlock the identity of the church, and the unity of brotherhood found in Ezekiel 37. "Can these bones live?"

CHAPTER 8

Silence in Heaven, and then...

Verse 1: *"And when he had opened the seventh seal, there was silence in heaven about the space of half an hour."*

We have studied the seals in Revelation being opened by Christ revealing the Spirit of the Lord in many facets. Let us re-read Isaiah 11: 1-5:

"And there shall come forth a rod out of the stem of Jesse, and a Branch shall grow out of his roots: and the spirit of the Lord shall rest upon him, the spirit of wisdom and understanding, the spirit of counsel and might, the spirit of knowledge and of the fear of the Lord; and shall make him of quick understanding in the fear of the Lord: and he shall not judge after the sight of his eyes, neither reprove after the hearing of his ears: But with righteousness shall he judge the poor, and reprove with equity for the meek of the earth: and he shall smite the earth with the rod of his mouth, and with the breath of his lips shall he slay the wicked. And righteousness shall be the girdle of his loins, and faithfulness the girdle of his reins."

Reiterating what we studied earlier; Isaiah is talking about Jesus as the rod, and humanity is the branch. It is the Christ in us that is opening the seal of our true identity, and the Spirit of the Lord in us is being revealed. These seven seals in Revelation are not literal, but symbolic of the number for rest or completeness in God.

The one who opened the seventh seal is the Christ or the Lamb of God slain in Chapter 4. Notice the verse says "had opened." This is more than the man Jesus who walked on the earth over two thousand years ago. This Christ was formed before the foundations of the world; before Genesis 1. When Jesus died on the cross, his body died with him. The corporate Christ is Jesus (the head) AND the body (all humanity). It is the corporate Christ who "had opened" the seventh seal.

John uses the word "hour" in his other books to reference a time in the life of Jesus that a miracle or the revelation of His identity had taken place. The half hour is symbolic of the time when our true identity as part of the corporate body of Christ is revealed. Jesus has fulfilled all that the "head of Christ" needed to do. He fulfilled all of it at Calvary. His death, burial, and resurrection completed the spring feast, but He also completed the Day of Atonement in the fall. How did He do this? In Hebrew understand there were two calendars used for measuring time. One was known as the Hebrew calendar which acknowledged the Feast Days of the Lord beginning in the month of Nisan as given to Moses. The other calendar was known as the civil calendar which identified the beginning of time as was known in the Scriptures. This began in the fall with the Feast Day of the Lord known as Rosh Hashanah or Yom Terrur. These calendars over-laid on each other, so that what was happening on Passover was also having a significance in time of 6 months later, yet coming to past in the now. The High Priest did not go into the Holy of Holies on Passover. This was not part of the custom and ritual. He only went into the Holy of Holies once a year on the Day of Atonement in the fall. Yet, Jesus became our High Priest at Passover once and for all.

During the time of Jesus, the folding of a napkin spoke a hidden meaning that the people would have understood. It was symbolic that a person had been in this place; completed the meal or task; and would not be returning. A Jewish woman would be shamed if her guest folded their dinner napkin after a meal. Jesus left a message for the disciples with a folded face cloth that was separate from the linens that his body had been wrapped in. There is another part of Christ that must come into unity. It is the body. *"The napkin that was about his head, not lying with the linen clothes, but wrapped together in a place by itself"* (John 20:7). The Passover meal has been finished. There is nothing more that Jesus needs to finish for humanity to come into the presence of God. It is time for the body to come into the manifestation of the finished work of Christ.

Verse 2: *"And I saw the seven angels which stood before God; and to them were given seven trumpets."*

The number seven used twice in this verse is not literal. It means perfection, complete, finished in God. There are more than seven angels or messengers before God. These are the mature in Christ. The trumpets symbolize the word of God coming out from the messengers. Throughout Scripture, when Jesus would use the word "behold," it was as a trumpet sounding with a declaration from God. The same message Jesus gave is being spoken, but coming through different vessels. Each vessel is declaring the word of God the way God has given it to them; but it is the same message and it brings unity and oneness to the body of Christ. The message is: "CHRIST IN YOU; THE HOPE OF GLORY" (Col. 1:27).

Having faith in God is our birthright we receive as born again believers in Jesus Christ. Walking that faith in God comes from our wilderness experience to Pentecost or receiving the Holy Spirit who releases the blessings of the Father.

Verse 3: *"And another angel came and stood at the altar, having a golden censer; and there was given unto him much incense, that he should offer it* *with the prayers of all saints upon the golden altar which was before the throne.*"

This other angel is Jesus. The "golden censer" is Christians. The "incense" represents prayers of an anointed nature that have a perfumed fragrance. Not all prayers that are spoken to God are anointed. In order for them to be lifted up to God, they must have an aroma that is pleasing to Him. Jesus was the mediator between God and man. *"For there is one God, and one mediator between God and men, the man Christ Jesus"* (1 Timothy 2:5). Hebrews 12: 24 tells us the same thing, *"And to Jesus the mediator of the new covenant."*

The altar of Incense was located before the Holy of Holies in the middle court or Holy Place. There were seven pieces of furniture required to be part of the temple of God. These pieces of furniture were arranged throughout the three courts in the shape of a cross. This altar would have been located in the center of the cross representing where the heart of Jesus would have been while he hung on the cross.

The "golden altar" and "throne" are symbolic of God and the Ark of the Covenant, or mercy seat of God. When we pray, our prayers go through our mediator, Jesus Christ, who transforms them to be presented in accordance to the will of God. Many of our prayers are unacceptable because they are self-centered. We can know they are "ego" oriented if they focus on looking for God to do something. God is not going to redo what He has already completed. Prayers that are acceptable to God are the prayers of faith which save (James 5:15). *"The effectual fervent prayer of a righteous man availed much"* (James 5:16). This faith is our faith in God, not how much faith we have in ourselves. The Holy Spirit intercedes with our prayers transforming them into His image and likeness. When we do not know how to pray, *"The Spirit makes intercession for us with groaning which cannot be uttered. And he* (Jesus) *that searcheth the hearts knoweth what is the mind of the spirit, because he maketh intercession for the saints according to the will of God."* (Romans 8:26-27). All three of the Godhead are working together to bring forth the predestined purpose and will of God. We are not to bring vain oblations, sacrifices or prayer requests to God (Isaiah 1:13). Since God's will has already been completed, it is now up to us to appropriate His will to come forth.

Many born again believers do not know that the will of God is found in the Torah, His teachings and instructions of the Old Testament. The mind of God is found in the written word, the Torah. This is where we find God's Divine plan. Our hardened hearts and iniquities of our forefathers passed down to us have kept us from the unveiling of the Truth. However, through Jesus Christ who took away the law of sin and death at Calvary, and gave us resurrection Life, we now have access to the blessings of the Father in the Torah because of His Love, not because of sin. The Father is not looking for our perfection in His Word. This was accomplished in Jesus Christ who IS the WORD, the Torah, made flesh. As we partake of His blood and His body through the Eucharist/communion/Sabbath we identify ourselves with Him in our earthen vessels as the living epistles, the Torah of God alive in the world.

Verse 4: *"And the smoke of the incense which came with the prayers of the saints, ascended up before God out of the angel's hand."*

The "smoke of the incense" is our prayers that we pray to God. Even though our prayers may not line-up with the right words, or may be self-centered, Jesus Christ is our intercessor. His ministry, represented by the hand, was responsible for searching our hearts for what we are really requesting from God through prayer. David says it in Psalm 141: 1-3, *"Lord, I cry unto thee: make haste unto me; give ear unto my voice, when I cry unto thee. Let my prayer by set forth before thee as incense; and the lifting up of my hands as the evening sacrifice. Set a watch, O Lord, before my mouth; keep the door of my lips."* As His body, Christ in us connects with the mind of Jesus Christ, sending forth the prayers of a righteous man that will avail much.

Verse 5: *"And the angel took the censer, and filled it with fire of the altar, and cast it into the earth: and there were voices, and thundering, and lightning, and an earthquake."*

Jesus Christ took the mature in Christ and they were filled with the Holy Spirit. The "earth" represents our flesh; fire represents the Holy Spirit; and the altar is the place of God. The "voices" are the mature in Christ; "thundering" is the word of God being spoken; "lightning" is God Himself speaking; an "earthquake" is the shaking of the mind. This is a picture of when the Christ in each of us is awakened to the mind of Christ for the corporate body. We will go through a shaking of our natural understanding that we will not comprehend; yet, it will speak so loud in our spirit that nothing else will be able to interrupt what God is saying.

This awakening began on the day of Pentecost found in Acts Chapter Two. The people were of one mind, and in one place, when suddenly a rushing mighty wind came from heaven and filled the house where everyone was at rest. They all spoke with another language that the Holy Spirit gave them. Even though they did not understand themselves, it was God speaking through them. Jesus said in Luke 12: 49, *"I am come to send fire on the earth."* In Mark 9: 49-50 we read, *"For every one shall be salted with fire, and every sacrifice shall be salted with salt. Salt is good: but if the salt have lost his saltiness, wherewith will ye season it? Have salt in yourselves, and have peace one with another."*

Jesus told His disciples before He died on the cross that He would meet them again in Galilee. He said this again to the women that met Him at the garden tomb. *"But after I am risen again, I will go before you into Galilee"* (Matthew 26:32). *"Then said Jesus unto them, Be not afraid: go tell my brethren that they go into Galilee, and there shall they see me"* (Matthew 28:10. Have you ever asked yourself why Galilee? From Jerusalem to the Galilee it is about a four days journey. Since the Old Testament ritual of Passover to Pentecost that was commanded by God for them to be in Jerusalem for these feast days, it was not common for people to travel very far outside of the Jerusalem boundaries. Going to the Galilee by foot would be at least an eight day journey round trip or longer because of not traveling on the Sabbath.

Included in this thought, we must consider the two disciples Jesus met on resurrection day traveling on the road to Emmaus which was NOT in the direction of the Galilee. Jesus meets them first as a Stranger from Jerusalem, shares the entire Old Testament with them, breaks bread with them, then disappears. We know the name of one of the disciples is Cleopas found in Luke 24. In John 19:25, we read that Cleopas had a wife named Mary who witnessed Jesus hanging on the cross with the other women. *"Now there stood by the cross of Jesus his mother, and his mother's sister, **Mary the wife of Cleopas**, and Mary Magdalene."*

Women are rarely mentioned with significance in the Scriptures and even more so as an equal to a man, yet here she is just as significant as an eye witness to the cross as John, and the other Mary's we are familiar with in Jesus's circle of disciples. When Luke tells his version it would be reasonable to assume that both Cleopas and his wife were the two disciples leaving Jerusalem for a day's journey to Emmaus when half way there they met a stranger they did not recognize as Jesus because they did not recognize the resurrected WORD of God in the flesh.

This is layered through going back in time to Genesis 3 with the man and woman in the garden conversing with a strange voice from the Tree of Knowledge of Good and Evil. *"And it came to pass, as he sat at meat with them, he took bread, and blessed it, and brake, and gave to them. And their eyes were opened, and they knew him; and he vanished out of their sight. And they said one to another, did not our heart burn within us, while he talked with us by the way, and while he opened to us the scriptures?"* (Luke 24:30-32). Mankind, in the image of male and female, heard and saw from their hearts, the throne room of the mercy seat of God the living tablets of stone. They heard the voice of God from the Tree of Life and took it back to Jerusalem where the other eleven disciples were dealing with so much fear they forgot that Jesus said He would meet them in Galilee, a four day journey. This was all necessary to fulfill not only the Passover Feast, but in the same season the Feast of unleavened bread and First Fruit BEFORE the church could be witnessed to by the voice of God in the upper room in Jerusalem on Pentecost. They needed to go to Galilee, remember all that Jesus said and miracles He did in the area, then slowly travel back to Jerusalem with the Resurrected Christ Jesus while "counting the omer" from Passover to Pentecost/Shavuot or the giving of the marriage covenant of God, the Torah.

"A new heart also will I give you, and a new spirit will I put within you: and I will take away the stony heart out of your flesh, and I will give you an heart of flesh" (Ezekiel 36:26). *"For this is the covenant that I will make with the house of Israel after those days, saith the Lord; I will put my laws into their mind, and write them in their hearts: and I will be to them a God, and they shall be to me a people"* (Hebrews 8:10).

Verse 6: *"And the seven angels which had the seven trumpets prepared themselves to sound."*

The key words in this verse are "prepared themselves." To be a vessel that God can speak through we must have an intimate relationship of love with God knowing Him as Father and Daddy. We cannot do the Father's business if we rely on others to tell us about God and we don't know Him personally.

Think about a relationship between a husband and wife. If their relationship focuses on physical intimacy alone, and not on developing together as one mind; after awhile, the physical side of their relationship will diminish also. The same thing happens in a relationship between parents and their children. If a person believes that being a good parent only revolves putting a roof over their children's head, food on the table, buying stylish clothes, and getting them to school; there will be a major awakening when the parents try to communicate with their children and they do not understand their thoughts and emotions. Somewhere in the life of the children there was not time given to get to know them as a unique individuals whom God created to bring unity and love into their home.

This is what many people miss in their relationship with God. They do not know Him as Father. Many who do consider God as Father still see Him as an adopted Father instead of their true Father. They do not consider themselves in the same class possessing His DNA (Luke 3:38). Religion wants us to believe that there is something we have to do, like say a "sinner's pray," in order to become children of God. Yet, Scripture reveals to us that we are already His children. In the Father's eyes, our identity as children was never removed; however, it was veiled from our understanding affecting our soul and physical life. What Jesus reconciled to us that Adam lost was the ability to have an intimate "Daddy and child" relationship. Our understanding of His love for us never ended and never will drawing us to an eternal perfect relationship that causes us to become mature as Jesus demonstrated as the First fruit of many first fruits today.

The writers of the New Testament wrote from a Hebraic understanding of Jesus Christ as the Messiah fulfilling the prophesies found in the Old Testament or Tanakh. The bloodline birthright and blessings comes to all the children of Abraham via the twelve tribes of Israel, not just the tribe of Judah known as the Jews. There is a direct DNA connection bone to bone and flesh to flesh. The Greek theologian uses the terminology of being grafted in as we do in the word adoption in western society. We can adopt a child, but that child would not have our blood DNA. This becomes a problem when we believe that the blood of Jesus has the ability to cleanse us from all unrighteousness if the life of the flesh is in blood. The Hebraic understanding is applicable, but the Greek thought is not.

Verse 7: *"The first angel sounded, and there followed hail and fire mingled with blood, and they were cast upon the earth: and the third part of trees was burnt up, and all green grass was burnt up."*

The angel in this verse and the ones to follow is symbolic of the completion of the work of Jesus Christ at Calvary: Jesus is the head of Christ, and we are the body. The Christ in us must first sound the finished work individually and then corporately. Remember an earthquake just occurred in verse 6, which is the shaking of all natural understanding in our lives. Following the shaking is "hail" which is frozen water. Hail reveals those partial truths or lies that we have wrongly attributed to God. Hail symbolizes the absoluteness of God's word.

"For whom he did foreknow, he also did predestinate to be conformed to the image of his Son, that he might be the firstborn among many brethren" (Romans 8:29)

When we first get a revelation from God that truly shakes our natural understanding, it is a "hard word" like a rod of iron. It is unchanging and uncompromising. John gave us the picture of the word being like hail coming down from the sky and beating us as it falls.

With hail, we have "fire." Fire is symbolized as cleansing and purifying. We also have "blood." Blood symbolizes LIFE. The life of the flesh is in the blood. When our flesh has been shaken, beaten, and then purified, the only life that remains is Christ found through the blood of Jesus. His identity is our identity.

Earthquake – shaking of the mind
Hail – hard core truth made known
Fire – purifying, refining, removing junk
Blood – LIFE in the flesh

Jesus Christ started the transformation process of revealing our true identity in Him. The angels, or messengers, who are the mature in Christ, are responsible to continue the transformation as vessels of His body until the fullness of the corporate body of Christ is revealed.

These messengers, or people, have an apostle's heart to prepare themselves with the word of God, or trumpet sound of the shofar that was heard on Mount Sinai. The earth represents a double-minded or carnal Christian, and the sea represents a spirit-filled Christian that is full of an earthly mind. They are being tossed around trying to cast out evil everywhere they go looking for the devil that they perceive is out to get everyone. As the mature in Christ are preparing themselves in the Lord the earthly, self-man will be removed. The only one left in us is the life of Christ.

Therefore, we have hail, fire, blood cast upon the earth, which is humanity, and one-third of the trees and grass were burnt up. This is symbolic of humanity and our natural thinking. It is not about people themselves, but about the way they are thinking which is opposed to the ways of God. God is not out to destroy us, but is correcting the way we use our hearts and minds towards one another. The one-third represents the outer court of the temple of God. Remember, there is an outer court

> *There is a difference between the words judgment and justice. Justice in Hebrew means: good deed, acts of loving kindness. "By me kings' reign, and princes decree justice." (Proverbs 8:15).*

that is symbolic of Passover, a middle court referring to Pentecost, and an inner court symbolic of Tabernacles. When we get to chapter 11 of Revelation, John was told to measure the temple of God. However, he is not supposed to measure the outer court. This is where the sacrifice of the Lamb took place for all humanity. Since Jesus died once for all we are not to judge anyone or else that same judgment will be used against us (Matthew 7:1-2). After all, we are all one in Him.

Verse 8: *"And the second angel sounded, and as it were a great mountain burning with fire was cast into the sea; and the third part of the sea became blood;"*

Mountains refer to a place of comprehension that is higher than our natural understanding. Fire represents God for He is a consuming fire. These messengers are speaking the word of God from the inner court with the power of His authority. Their words are being directed to the middle court or those that refer to themselves as being spirit-filled believers. Some of the most dangerous people in the body of Christ can be spirit-filled or Pentecostal believer. They get a little revelation and mix it with humanity; then go around preaching a judgmental message that gives places to devils and demons, or the psychic realm with a voice that says "thus says the Lord" when the Lord never said it in the heart content that is being portrayed. When the word of truth comes to these people their humanity, or natural way of understanding, will be removed. Again, the life of Christ will remain.

Often times when the Spirit of the Lord is leading we are so eager to know what He is doing that we get ahead of God creating a mixture of truth that becomes a playground for the enemy of God.

Verse 9: *"And the third part of the creatures which were in the sea, and had life, died; and the third part of the ships were destroyed."*

The word "creatures" is creation. Remember sea is not a literal large body of water, but symbolic of believers that know the word of God, yet have mixed it with their natural understanding. The creation that was formed with their imagination must go. God will not share His life with anyone or any other creation. The word "life" is "psuche" referring to our soul life, not spirit. We must die to ourselves so that the life that we now live is by the faith of the Son of God (Gal. 2:20). This is not how much faith we have, but the faith of Christ Jesus in us released through us by His Holy Spirit.

We, the church, are the side of Christ or His body as the woman that was taken from the side of Adam. We are bone of His bone and flesh of His flesh today. It was the side of Jesus that the Roman soldier speared and blood and water came out. Scripture tells us to let the mind of Christ that was in Jesus also be our mind (Phil. 2:5). The mind that Jesus had was "Christ" meaning God, and "Jesus" meaning man. Jesus Christ was God-Man. This is the same mind that we are commanded to have *"if we be Christ's"* (Gal. 3:29).

The word "ships" is symbolic of the different systems of humanity. Each of us is a vessel of the Lord's body carrying the Word of God. When we try to do something for the Lord that is not His desire for us, our ship will be torpedoed. Many times, we build large ships giving those names of denominations or doctrines, yet they are not of God. Just like the Tower of Babel, God will come down and make His presence known allowing us to refocus on Him who is really in control.

Remember in Genesis 11, where God changed the communication to cause confusion and disrupt their unity in self-focus? He did not have to literally kill the people. The power of life and death is in the tongue (Proverbs 18:21). In God's timing for each of us, we will all bow to the name of Jesus whether we are in heaven, in the earth, or under the earth; and we will all confess that Jesus Christ is Lord to the glory of God the Father (Phil. 2:10-11). The humanitarian part of us that

"In the beginning God created the heaven and the earth (everything). And the earth (temple for God identity to reside in) was without form, and void; and darkness was upon the face (identity) of the deep (creation, imagination). And the Holy Spirit moved upon the face of the waters (life giving source). God said, Let there be light: and there was light (His identity)." Genesis 1:1-3

we have had in the outer court, or Passover, must be destroyed. Any part of "self" that we may try to bring into the middle court, or Pentecost, will also be destroyed. Remember, this is individually, then corporately the body of Christ being formed in the womb of the earth that belongs to God as the believer allows the working of the salvation to work through them in the midst of trials and tribulations that oppose the WORD of God.

Verse 10: *"And the third angel sounded, and there fell a great star from heaven, burning as it were a lamp, and it fell upon the third part of the rivers and upon the fountains of water;"*

The great star from heaven is Christ. Jesus who is our Bright and Morning Star (Rev. 22:16). The word "fell" is symbolic of His crucifixion, which took place for us. We contain the rivers and fountains of waters. *"The words of a man's mouth are as deep waters and the wellspring of wisdom as a flowing brook"* (Proverbs 18:4). *"He that believeth on me, as the Scripture hath said, out of his belly shall flow rivers of living water"* (John 7:38).

The mind of Christ fell upon the earth, the male/female created in the image of God (Genesis 1:28), and God purified the words they spoke. The "Lamp" is symbolic of Light. *"God is Light, and in Him is no darkness"* (1 John 1: 5). Fire is a purifier. God is a consuming Fire (Hebrews 12:29), and it is *"He that goeth over before thee; as a consuming fire He shall destroy them, and He shall bring them down before thy face:"* (Deut. 9:3). We cannot purify ourselves. God will come upon the mind and heart of man and the Spirit of Christ in man will witness to the presence of God bringing transformation in each of us.

Verse 11: *"And the name of the star is called Wormwood: and the third part of the waters became wormwood; and many men died of the waters, because they were made bitter."*

This verse is full of symbolism. We have the great Star signifying Jesus Christ now called Wormwood. In the Hebrew, the word wormwood is "la-anah" meaning "a root that is cursed or poisonous." In the Greek, it is the word "absinthes" meaning "uncertain derivation, bitterness, and calamity." Before Jesus went to the cross, He cursed the fig tree to the root which represented Israel. It was not producing fruit out of season anymore. This is not about a literal fruit tree, but taking the Torah and using it to justify

Jesus cursed the fig tree before He went to Calvary, to signify that the fruit from the Tree of Knowledge of Good and Evil would not be the identity of the people of God anymore.

good and evil. The words of a believer are the fruit of the body of Christ that have the ability to create just as the first Adam was brought "form" for him to label for eternity. Adam gave the names of the animals, but he was never to give names to the image of God that would take eternity and lock the name in time with a separate image apart from God. When Jesus hung on the cross, David described His anguish in Psalm 22:6 as, *"I am a worm, and no man; a reproach of men, and despised of the people."*

Trees are symbolic of humanity. Jesus became as "wormwood," the root of sin, crucified and destroyed for all humanity. The curse or bitterness of humanity was the law of sin and death, not the Torah of God, His teachings and instructions as a Father to His children. *"Christ hath redeemed us from the curse of the law, being made a curse* (wormwood) *for us: for it is written, Cursed is everyone that hangeth on a tree* (cross)" (Galatians 3:13).

The third part of the waters represents the part of our thinking that is still in the outer court or Passover realm. This is the part in each of us where we still have bitterness, anger, irritation, and indignation instead of the springs of life flowing out of our belly. Remember, there is life and death in our words. Our words really can hurt others causing a bitterness that only the love of God can forgive and heal.

Verse 12: *"And the fourth angel sounded, and the third part of the sun was smitten, and the third part of the moon, and the third part of the stars; so as the third part of them was darkened, and the day shone not for a third part of it, and the night likewise."*

The number four is a universal number. This is a message for all humanity around the world – north, south, east, and west of Jerusalem. The message is going to the realm of our understanding that is surrounded by sacrifice. The High Priest at First Fruit would wave a sheath of Barley which is for cleansing the body, so that the radiance of Christ in us would be seen to our north, south, east, and west waved to the outer court of the temple of God. The reference to the sun, moon, and stars takes us to Genesis 37 where Joseph has a dream. His father, Jacob, interprets the dream as the sun being himself (Jacob), the moon being his wife (Joseph's mother), and the stars his brothers that will bow down to Joseph. Joseph is a type of Jesus. *"At the name of Jesus every knee should bow, of things in heaven, and things in earth, and things under the earth; and that every tongue should confess that Jesus Christ is Lord, to the glory of God the Father."* (Phil. 2:10-11).

> *Jesus finished it ALL. He is waiting for the Father's permission to come for His bride, His body, to consummate His marriage as one new man/Adam in the earth. The bride must be His voice, His nature, His essence now.*

Darkness is not necessarily bad, but a manifestation of ignorance in understanding God. In Genesis 1:2-4, *"And the earth was without form, and void; and darkness was upon the face of the deep. And the Spirit of God moved upon the face of the waters. And God said, Let there be light: and there was light. And God saw the light, that it was good: and God divided the light from the darkness."* God did not destroy darkness, but moved upon it to reveal the light, or god identity in the midst of the darkness that was already there to shine brighter. A third part of the temple of God will be in darkness or understanding of Christ.

This is just a temporary moment of God's timing, but eventually all will come into the presence and understanding of the love of God. Remember what we read in the paragraph above; every knee shall bow and confess that Jesus Christ is Lord. Love prompts us to make that confession, not condemnation. Romans 8:1, *"There is therefore now no condemnation to them which are in Christ Jesus."* We love Him because He first loved us!

Verse 13: *"And I beheld and heard an angel flying through the midst of heaven, saying with a loud voice, Woe, woe, woe, to the inhabiters of the earth by reason of the other voices of the trumpet of the three angels, which are yet to sound!"*

The word "beheld" is the word "saw," and the word "midst" is referring to within each of us. Heaven is not off in the sky somewhere, but within us. We are the heaven that God dwells in, where this spirit/ messenger is flying in the midst of. The Holy Spirit within us is saying, *"Woe, woe, woe"* which literally means; pain, grief, and suffering *"to the inhabiters of the earth."* Those that inhabit the earth realm are comfortable in the first two courts: Passover or outer court people are like dust; and the Pentecost or middle court people are like sand. Those who exist in these realms have a covenant relationship with God, but are limited to what the earth offers in their understanding. Dust and sand are serpent's food.

Outer court (Passover realm) characteristics that produce "woe" include the belief that we are saved by grace, yet still sinners by nature; and the notion that we should primarily be concerned about our own salvation. Middle court (Pentecost realm) characteristics that produce "woe" believe that we have it all being spirit-filled; believing we must cast out devils whenever something goes wrong; and believing there is an eternal hell for non-believers. Isaiah tells us in 55: 8-9, *"For my thoughts are not your thoughts, neither are your ways my ways, saith the Lord. For as the heavens are higher than the earth, so* are my ways higher than your ways, and my thoughts than your thoughts." This is a place within us that we can choose to rest.

Paul says in Ephesians 1: 3, *"Blessed be the God and Father of our Lord Jesus Christ, who hath blessed us with all spiritual blessings in heavenly places in Christ"* …Eph. 2: 5-6, *"Even when we were dead in sins, hath quickened us together with Christ, (by grace ye are saved;) and hath raised us up together, and made us sit together in heavenly places in Christ Jesus."*

Isaiah is experiencing the ALL of God available to us as we move from the Holy Place into the Holy of Holies. We love God at the Shabbat of braking bread and drinking wine, but now it is time to Love Him as a wife.

Many people are satisfied with just "being saved." This mindset is connected to the outer court or Passover realm in the temple of God. Others are content to be connected with the middle court or Pentecost realm by considering they are Spirit-Filled because they have a prayer language with the ability to pray in other tongues. The Pentecost Feast is the celebration of preparing one's heart to receive the Father's teachings and instructions by the Holy Spirit in one accord with the body of Christ, not just a prayer language.

There is an inner court of the temple of God known as Tabernacle celebrated as The Lord's Feast of Sukkot. This is the consummation of oneness with God in the Holy of Holiness to produce more children of God, the WORD impregnated in the bride/wife of Christ, to be moved by the Holy Spirit upon the face of the deep in the womb. Then in the fullness of time to be a fountain of living water out of the inner most belly. Spring forth to the heart of circumcision and give life as the WORD is released through the tongue. Even those that have entered this realm have not received the fullness available because this realm is filled with eternity. The supply of God's availability never stops and is located within each of us.

The remaining voices of the trumpet of the three angels yet to sound are the eternal word of God. Those in Tabernacle do not experience the "woes." It is for those that are content to remain in the dust and the sand instead of coming into the heavens where we are to be seated in Christ. The carnal mind cannot ascend into the heavens for flesh and blood cannot inherit the Kingdom of God (1 Corinthians 15:50). *"Even the very dust of your city, which cleaveth on us, we do wipe off against you: notwithstanding be ye sure of this, that the kingdom of God is come nigh unto you"* (Luke 10:11). *"The kingdom of God cometh not with observation: neither shall they say, Lo here! Or, lo there! For, behold, the kingdom of God is within you"* (Luke 17:20-21).

Ecclesiastes 3:1 says, *"To every thing there is a season, and a time to every purpose UNDER the heaven"*... Verse 11: *"he hath made every thing beautiful in His time: also he hath set the world* (eternity) *in their heart, so that no man can find out the work that God maketh from the beginning to the end."*... Verse 15: *"That which hath been is NOW; and that which is to be hath already been; and God requireth that which is past."*

When we have come into Tabernacle or the presence of God we will hear the messengers cry out *"Holy, holy, holy, is the Lord of hosts: the whole earth is full of his glory"* (Isaiah 6:3). When Isaiah heard this he said in verse 5, *"Woe is me! For I am undone; because I am a man of unclean lips, and I dwell in the midst of a people of unclean lips: for mine eyes have seen the King, the Lord of hosts."* Isaiah tried to take himself, a natural man, into the Holy of Holies. What happened next in verses 6-8: *"Then flew one of the seraphim* (messengers that come suddenly and boldly like a snake striking a person) *unto me, having a live coal* (the consuming fire of God) *in his hand* (5-fold ministry) *which he had taken with the tongs* (finger

"And I heard a great voice out of heaven saying, Behold, the tabernacle of God is with men, and he will dwell with them, and they shall be his people, and God himself shall be with them, and be their God" (Revelation 21:3).

of God) *from off the altar* (this is the altar of incense before the Holy of Holies filled with the praises of God and forgiveness towards all mankind). *And he laid it upon my mouth* (life and death are in the power of the tongue) *and said, Lo, this hath touched thy lips; and thine iniquity is taken away, and thy sin purged. Also I heard the voice of the Lord, saying, whom shall I send, and who will go for us? Then said I, Here am I; send me* (I can do the business of the Father like Jesus did because I now see myself as a son of God)."

So what was the business that God had Isaiah do? Verse 9-10: *"And He said, Go, and tell this people, Hear ye indeed, but understand not; and see ye indeed, but perceive not. Make the heart of this people fat* (filled with unconditional love of God), *and make their ears heavy* (so they only hear the love, mercy, and forgiveness of God without any condition with it), *and shut their eyes* (so they see no evil); *lest they see with their eyes* (God's eyes), *and hear with their ears* (God's ears), *and understand with their heart* (His heart) *and convert* (their true identity created in His image), *AND BE HEALED."*

Each time Jesus revealed heaven to people, he took them aside, away from the crowd. Afterwards he would tell them not to tell anyone. This is different from what we see taking place in our "mega" churches. Heaven (Holy of Holies or Tabernacle realm) has no place for emotionalism or self-identity. It is only God, and His image or identity, which can be in this place.

The Hebrew understanding of the word Tabernacles had a picture image where the children of God created small booths to stay in outside like camping under the stars. It was a finished season of reading the Torah scrolls from Genesis to Deuteronomy. It was a time of gathering and ingathering of wheat, barley and all the blessings of the vine. It was a time of great celebration. The first nail for creating the booths was placed at sundown at the completion of Yom Kippur – the Day of Atonement. Jesus was fulfilling the civil calendar of the fall feast days of the Lord while He was manifesting the completion of the spring feast days of the Biblical calendar. The nails were being removed from His body symbolizing that the Tabernacle of God is not a physical booth made of wood and branches, but a life giving place within mankind that has prepared themselves as His bride.

Jesus said in Luke 10: 21-24,

> *"In that hour Jesus rejoiced in spirit, and said, I thank thee, O Father, Lord of heaven and earth, that thou hast hid these things from the wise and prudent, and hast revealed them unto babes: even so, Father; for so it seemed good in thy sight. All things are delivered to me of my Father: and no man knoweth who the Son is, but the Father; and who the Father is, but the Son, and he to whom the Son will reveal him. And he turned him unto his disciples, and said privately, Blessed are the eyes which see the things that ye see: For I tell you, that many prophets and kings have desired to see those things which ye see, and have not seen them, and to hear those things which ye hear, and have not heard them."*

To grow in Christ, we must be willing to let go of our natural understanding. Those that are in the world will go through Passover in God's timing. It is by the love of God released through the Holy Spirit in us that mankind is drawn to the Father to hear how to have a relationship with the Divine presence of God as a family member. Other religions can show the world how to respect and honor God, but Jesus alone showed us that God is our Heavenly Father.

Those hanging around Passover and sin sacrifices must let go and move into Pentecost when the Holy Spirit stirs within them. Then in His timing again, those in Pentecost or "spirit-filled" understanding will move beyond the veil into the Holy of Holies or Tabernacle. Moving into Tabernacle is a one on one experience with God. There must be a hunger for the Father's teachings and instructions found in the Old Testament. This is the oil in the lamp that the five wise virgins had. This is an individual desire, not something you can share which is why the five foolish virgins had to go back to Pentecost to receive the fullness of the Father's teachings in the Torah. They missed the bridegroom. They were not ready but still in a preparation stage.

Matthew 25:1-10:

> *"Then shall the kingdom of heaven be likened unto ten virgins, which took their lamps, and went forth to meet the bridegroom. And five of them were wise, and five were foolish. They that were foolish took their lamps, and took no oil with them: But the wise took oil in their vessels with their lamps. While the bridegroom tarried, they all slumbered and slept. And at midnight there was a cry made, Behold, the bridegroom cometh; go ye out to meet him. Then all those virgins arose, and trimmed their lamps. And the foolish said unto the wise, give us of your oil; for our lamps are gone out. But the wise answered, saying, not so; lest there be not enough for us and you: but go ye rather to them that sell, and buy for yourselves. And while they went to buy, the bridegroom came; and they that were ready went in with him to the marriage: and the door was shut."*

It is just you and Him at the Alter of Incense, and then just HIM. You do not exist in Tabernacles. Paul explains this in 1Timothy 1:5, *"Now the end of the commandment is charity* (unconditional love, mercy, and forgiveness that only God can give) *out of a pure heart, and of a good conscience, and of faith unfeigned* (the finished work of Jesus Christ).

Passover is being born again as a new creation in Christ Jesus. Your identity was always there in your DNA, but the enemy had sold you a lie.

Pentecost is receiving the Torah, the Father's teaching and instructions to mature in Christ as a son of God able to do the Father's business in the earth.

Tabernacles is the oneness of Jesus Christ and the church that is the bride who has prepared herself to carry His name, nature, and essence ruling and reigning with Him in the world. The new man! *"For he himself is our peace, who has made the two groups – male/female – one and has destroyed the barrier, the dividing wall of hostility, by setting aside in his flesh the law of sin and death with its commands and regulations. His purpose was to create in himself one new humanity out of the two, thus making peace, and in one body, the bride of Christ, to reconcile both of them, male/female, to God through the cross, by which he put to death their hostility"* (Ephesians 2:14-16).

God finished Revelation BEFORE Genesis. Jesus was the Lamb slain BEFORE the foundation of the world. We are His body, and the manifestation of His LIFE is being revealed today in us as we allow the Holy Spirit to lead and guide us into all wisdom and truth of the Father's teachings and instructions.

Notes of Reflection

What were your immediate thoughts in this chapter?

_____

_____

_____

_____

_____

What preconceived thoughts did you have before reading this chapter?

_____

_____

_____

_____

_____

What new information did you learn?

_____

_____

_____

_____

_____

Does this information seem confusing or liberating? Why?

_____

_____

_____

_____

_____

CHAPTER 9

Final Trumpet Sounds

"And I beheld, and heard an angel flying through the midst of heaven, saying with a loud voice, Woe, woe, woe, to the inhabiters of the earth by reason of the other voices of the trumpet of the three angels, which are yet to sound!" (Revelation 8:13).

We begin again…another day…another chapter, yet part of the former because of the word "AND."

Verse One: *"And the fifth angel sounded and I saw a star fall from heaven unto the earth: and to him was given the key of the bottomless pit."*

The number five is symbolic for "grace." It is not the kind of fabricated grace that says "if you do this, then I will give you grace." The grace of God was given to each of us while we were still in ignorance and darkness. King James calls this darkness "sin." (Romans 8:5). The grace of God gives life

> *The grace of God did not begin with the church in Acts 2. It was first given to the children of God when they came out of Egypt in Exodus 37.*

overshadowing death releasing power to bring us out of darkness into His marvelous LIGHT and LIFE that we could not obtain on our own.

As we mentioned before in previous chapters, the angel is a messenger of God. An angel may be a human that has been given divine revelation to bring life, love, and light to another. It may be the manifestation of an angelic being (son of God) that has already gone before us who has been commissioned to bring a message to us by God, or it can be a heavenly creation of God that is neither man or beast. Nevertheless, the issue is not about the messenger, but the message.

The sound the angel is making is the blowing of a trumpet, or shofar. At this point, I would like to share some wisdom about this trumpet that I have already alluded to in previous chapters. There is only one trumpet being blown, yet symbolically each sound is distinct as if there were seven (Rev. 8:6). This trumpet is the sound of JUBILEE. It is made by blowing into a Ram's horn. Jesus was the Ram who was slain so that the sound of Jubilee could be known through him. A ram's horn represents a stubborn, dead beast, you and me, that now has the sound of the resurrection life of Christ Jesus coming out of our body.

Genesis 22:8, *"And Abraham said, my son,* **God will provide himself** *a lamb for a burnt offering: so they went both of them together."*…Genesis 22:13, *"And Abraham lifted up his eyes, and looked, and behold behind him a* **ram** *caught in a thicket by his horns: and Abraham went and took the* **ram***, and offered him up for a burnt offering in the stead of his son."*

This ram was not just a sacrificial lamb, but represented the finished work that Abraham believed in by faith to be seen in a coming day. Hebrews 11:12-13, *"Therefore sprang there even of one, and him as good as dead, so many as the stars of the sky in multitude, and as the sand which is by the sea shore innumerable. These all died in faith, not having received the promises, but having seen them afar off, and were persuaded of them, and embraced them, and confessed that they were strangers and pilgrims on the earth."*

As those in the Old Testament looked for a coming day of the Messiah by the faith of God, believers in Christ can now say, "Because of the

Lamb slain" my faith is in God's faithfulness and promises that I am today a new creation in Christ.

In the Old Testament, the people longed to hear this trumpet sound that would declare their jubilee. It was only heard once every 50 years on the Day of Atonement. However, the **sound** of the Ram's horn had to be heard. This day would come and the horn would be blown, but if the trumpet was not heard, jubilee would not come to that person. The Bible dictionary description of this time:

JUBILEE

At the close of the great Day of Atonement, the blast of the jubilee curved trumpets proclaimed throughout the land liberty, after guilt had been removed through the typically atoning blood of victims. It is referred to as antitypical fulfilled in "the acceptable year of the Lord," this limited period of gospel grace in which deliverance from sin and death, and the restoration of man's lost inheritance, are proclaimed through Christ (Isaiah 61:1-2; Luke 4:19). Literally, hereafter (Ezekiel 7:12-13; 46:17) to be kept. (From Fausset's Bible Dictionary, Electronic Database Copyright (c) 1998 by Biblesoft)

Jesus is our jubilee. Through Him, time and eternity became one. He is the star that fell from heaven in this first verse, which brought unconditional grace to the world at the time, which he was crucified on the cross. 2 Corinthians 8:7, *"Therefore, as ye abound in every thing, in faith, and utterance, and knowledge, and in all diligence, and in your love to us, see that ye abound in this grace also."*

> *The significance of this particular sound is first told in the Old Testament when it was the sound of the ram's horn heard by the children of God AS the voice of God on Mount Sinai.*

"A star fell from heaven unto the earth." The word "unto" can be read "into." The word "earth" is not only the literal natural realm that Jesus

came into, but also refers to our own flesh. We are earthen vessels that He has already come into so that we could dwell with Him and the Father. John 14:20, *"At that day ye shall know that I am in my Father, and ye in me, and I in you."*

"To him was given the key of the bottomless pit" A key represents power and authority. Without a key, you cannot unlock a door or start a car. Within each of our hearts, we hold the seed of our true identity as a son of God. *"He hath set the world* (eternity, His identity) *in their heart, so that no man can find out the work that God maketh from the beginning to the end"* (Ecclesiastes 3:11b).

We established that it was Jesus who has this key from Revelation 1:18, *"I am the Living One; I was dead, and behold I am alive for ever and ever! And I hold the keys of death and Hades."* Also in Matthew 28:18 we read,

"Then Jesus came to them and said, "All authority in heaven and on earth has been given to me." Jesus has power and authority over the bottomless pit. When we know that we are born again we are given ALL the dunamis, supernatural, Divine power that God place in the first Adam in Genesis 1 which was lost in Genesis 3. Jesus is telling us that He alone – not a devil – has ALL power and authority to give to whomever He chooses.

What is this bottomless pit? It is our imagination. Out of our natural understanding ascends any evil, fornication, adultery, uncleanness, lasciviousness, idolatry, witchcraft, hatred, variance, emulations, wrath, strife, seditions, heresies, envying, murders, drunkenness, and such like that Paul talks about in Galatians 5. Each time we blame a devil when these things happen we cheat ourselves from allowing the Holy Spirit to unlock the bondage of our imagination. This has been the problem since time began with Adam blaming the woman instead of being accountable before God.

The words of the woman spoken were first created in the heart of man/Adam before she was created separately. Adam/man was right there with the woman during the whole conversation she was having with the serpent. He could have corrected the conversation at any time for he alone heard directly from the Father not to eat of the Tree of Knowledge. She was separated from Adam after the conversation with God. This fruit are WORDS. The woman was having a conversation about the fruit of words, not apples or oranges. *"Death and life are in the power of the tongue: and they that love it shall eat the fruit thereof"* (Proverbs 18:21).

Notice that we do not have the key, but Christ in us does. Jesus removed the bondage to our understanding so that the Holy Spirit can now enlighten us. He is the way; He is the door. What is this key that has power and authority over our imagination? It is the unconditional grace, mercy, and love that our Heavenly Father has for each of us. Romans 5:8, *"But God commendeth his love toward us, in that, while we were yet sinners, Christ died for us."* This is what He wants us to give away to others, but we cannot do this if we do not believe it ourselves. We cannot be double-minded thinking we are "sinners saved by grace" and then think we can give away unconditional love. In this mindset, our love would be judgmental since it is the only kind of love we have allowed ourselves to receive. It takes the faith of God to believe in unconditional love, mercy, and grace. It takes the mind of Christ to see that sin and the "sinner" has been destroyed. Paul tells us in Philippians 2:5-6, *"Let this mind be in you, which was also in Christ Jesus: Who, being in the form of God, thought it not robbery to be equal with God:"* The Grace of God is more than unmerited favor for we find in Scripture that Jesus grew in wisdom and GRACE. *"And the child grew, and waxed strong in spirit, filled with wisdom: and the grace of God was upon him"* (Luke 2:4). He did not need unmerited favor for He is God in the flesh, perfect and sinless.

Grace is the equipping dunamis power of God that breaks the strongholds of our imagination. It draws us out of death into Life to receive the instructions from the Father to live Life in His heavenly abundance in the earth, not because of the wrath of God, but the because of the passion of His Love.

Verse 2: *"And He opened the bottomless pit; and there arose a smoke out of the pit, as the smoke of a great furnace and the sun and the air were darkened by reason of the smoke of the pit."*

We established what the bottomless pit was: our imagination. What is this smoke coming out? The smoke is humanity; the ignorance that humanity has in their mind. It was symbolized by the cherubim that were placed on the curtain between the Holy Place and the Holy of Holies in the Tabernacle of the Wilderness. These cherubim were created out of an Egyptian imagination. The Bible does not give any detail of what they were supposed to look like which is why different artists have different images of cherubim.

This imagery is connected with the children of Israel and their encounter with God on Mount Sinai. They had come out of Egypt, but Egypt had not come out of them. Right before the voice of God was heard by all, a great cloud descended upon the people so thick they could not see each other. There was to be NO imagination of what God looked like, but to have the senses of man focused on HEARING His voice.

"And mount Sinai was altogether on a smoke, because the LORD descended upon it in fire: and the smoke thereof ascended as the smoke of a furnace, and the whole mount quaked greatly. And when the voice of the trumpet sounded long, and waxed louder and louder, Moses spoke, and God answered him by a voice. And the LORD came down upon mount Sinai, on the top of the mount: and the LORD called Moses up to the top of the mount; and Moses went up" (Exodus 19:18-20). As the Holy Spirit, the fire of God, moves across our imagination, the imagination burns to ashes unveiling the beauty of Christ in us.

"To appoint unto them that mourn in Zion, to give unto them beauty for ashes, the oil of joy for mourning, the garment of praise for the spirit of heaviness; that they might be called trees of righteousness, the planting of the LORD, that he might be glorified" (Isaiah 61:3). Mount Zion is the place the disciples were told to go and wait for the Holy Spirit. The church began as a Pentecost/Shavuot celebration of the Lord's Feast Day, not the feast of Passover. Mount Zion is paralleled to the Mount Sinai experience. They had to leave Jerusalem and to the Galilee to meet Jesus as the Resurrection Life. Then, from the Galilee they spent the days from Passover to Pentecost journeying back to Jerusalem. These 50 days are known as counting the Omer. It was this season that Jesus was witnessed as the Resurrection Christ to over 500 people. *"He appeared to Cephas, and then to the Twelve. After that, he appeared to more than five hundred of the brothers and sisters at the same time, most of whom are still living, though some have fallen asleep. Then he appeared to James, then to all the apostles, and last of all he appeared to me also, as to one abnormally born"* (I Corinthian 15:5-8).

A hidden thought to consider that has caused misunderstandings through time can be found with the tradition of the High Priest entering the Holy of Holies on the Day of Atonement. The High Priest was supposed to meet with God in front of the mercy seat between the poles. This would allow the two Cherubim that are sitting on the mercy seat to be viewed facing each other bowing towards the middle of the

The cherubim on the Ark of the Covenant represents mankind as the messengers of God sitting on the mercy seat with Christ Jesus as High Priest on the Torah of God.

mercy seat. The High Priest was to be in that same position **between** the poles that carry the Ark of the Covenant.

If you take a look at many of our statues and icons that represent the Ark of the Covenant you will see the poles extended behind the cherubim. This position would place the High Priest facing the back of one of the cherubim instead of between them. If you do not know a little about Jewish history and go by most artists' drawings of the Ark of the Covenant, you would find the High Priest not able to meet with God between the poles. Most illustrations would force the High Priest to visit God behind one of the cherubim, or be in front of the mercy seat with no poles. What difference do the poles make? The poles represent being locked into God with His mercy, love, and forgiveness. Meeting with God between the poles in front of the mercy seat, with the curtain that separates spiritual and natural behind us, allows us to receive all that God has already given to us through Jesus Christ. You are totally wrapped in the ultimate spiritual hug from your heavenly Father. If you are viewing this from the backside of Cherubim, you will never receive the fullness of what the Father has to give. You will still have your "imagination" between you and God.

Cherubim represent the bottomless pit of what comes out of our natural thinking process. There is no end to it. Our natural understanding is an abomi**nation** to God. He hates, or detests this "nation" because it apposes everything that allows the truth of our inheritance as His children to be manifested. Romans 8:6-7, *"For to be carnally minded is death; but to be spiritually minded is life and peace. Because the carnal mind is enmity against God:"* Where does death begin? It is in the power of our tongue; Proverbs 18:21, *"Death and life are in the power of the tongue: and they that love it shall eat the fruit thereof."* What feeds the tongue? Matthew 15:17-18, *"Do not ye yet understand that whatsoever entereth in at the mouth goeth into the belly, and is cast out into the draught? But those things which proceed out of the mouth come forth from the heart; and they defile the man."*

Verse 2 of Revelation Chapter 9 gives the wisdom we need to follow in order to be released from the control of the imagination. This nation only causes a veil to cover our understanding, polluting the air around us to mask the fullness of our identity as sons of God. The following is the author's translation of this verse to help give some clarity:

"And Jesus unlocked the imagination of humanity; ignorance came out of man's natural understanding. The ignorance veiling and controlling mankind had polluted the air they breathed causing a screen between man and the light of the world that Jesus was releasing never to have dominion again."

Verse 3: *"And there came out of the smoke locusts upon the earth: and unto them was given power, as the scorpions of the earth have power."*

If I read this with my natural understanding, my immediate thought would be "where is the blessing I was told I would receive in Rev. 1:3?" In the natural, this does sound very fearful, but God is Spirit and so is His word!

"Came out of the smoke" speaks of the veil of man's ignorance being removed. The word "locust" does not refer to literal flying bugs, but is symbolic. The word means "to light on the top of." The word "upon" is the Greek word "eis" which means "into." These locusts are symbolic of something separating us from spiritually understanding what the Holy Spirit wants us to know. They are the destroying "ites" in Deuteronomy 7 that controls humanity. We have talked about these before in the chapter one of volume one of this study, but to refresh your understanding there were seven "ites" that had to be overcome by Moses and the children of God. They were:

- Hittites - violence
- Girgashites - lying
- Amorites - pride
- Canaanites - rebellion
- Perizzites - independent
- Hivites - fear
- Jebusites – religion

When we minister with our perception or temperament only, and don't allow the opportunity for the Holy Spirit to speak to us through others we set ourselves up for becoming a false prophet.

Humanity has unknowingly allowed these "ites" to return by giving them power that they do not legally have. Religious people (locust, or Christ mind destroyers) will use the word of God to try to control the Christ identity our heavenly Father has placed in each person's heart (Eccl. 3:11). When leaders in the church lead according to the way they alone hear from God, not allowing the Holy Spirit to speak in or through another because the message is coming a different way is actually a reflection of one of the horses we discussed in Chapter six of volume one of this study. Being spirit led does not mean the spirit man is being led by the temperament of man, but the temperament is silent so the Life of Christ in the temple is manifested.

The reference to "scorpions" has the word "as" before it. This is not literal scorpions running around with big stingers in their tail. This is a spiritual issue referring to demonic influence in our "earth" or in the life of a believer of Jesus Christ. The power of a scorpion is in the tail to sting. If we are stung enough by the "doom and gloom" around us, it can kill us. Scorpions were very prevalent in Egypt. Egypt is symbolic of our natural or worldly understanding. The tail of the scorpion is symbolic of "false prophets or false teachers." They are people that interpret God's word with literal understanding bringing judgment and condemnation to others instead of the life and love that Jesus illustrated.

People who preach by their carnal understanding lack a loving relationship with their Heavenly Father. Our Father is love, and we are created in His image with His blood. This is what Jesus came to show us. The Holy Spirit in us is releasing the bondage of the "sting of the scorpion" through the revelation of the word or "the light within us." Paul tells us the reason for this is, *"to make all men see what is the fellowship of the mystery, which from the beginning of the world hath been hid in God, who created all things by Jesus Christ"* (Ephesians 3:9); however, we must remember that it is also written in Proverbs 25:2, *"It is the glory of God to conceal a thing: but the honor of kings is to search out a matter."* If we do not grow up to be the kings and priests He made us to be (Rev. 1:6), we cannot expect to understand the wisdom of our Heavenly Father. Hence, we have many false prophets and teachers in the body of Christ giving us "the sting of the scorpion" through their carnal understanding of what the Bible says.

Verse 4: *"And it was commanded them that they should not hurt the grass of the earth, neither any green thing, neither any tree; but only those men which have not the seal of God in their foreheads."*

John is writing some wonderful symbolism in this verse. The Holy Spirit is commanding the carnal mind in us (locust) not to hurt any grass, green thing, or any tree. In 1 Peter 1:24 and Isaiah 40:6 and 8, we will find that the word "grass" means, "all flesh." When we receive revelation from God, it is not to be hurtful to anyone. It is supposed to edify and encourage bringing unity to the body.

The "green thing" refers to anything that has life: revelation knowledge given by the Holy Spirit will not destroy. Remember, we are talking spiritual, not literal. How many of us have been victims of having the word of God quoted to us to bring justification and condemnation stirring our emotions to be afraid that God was out to destroy us? This is what God means when He says, "don't harm anything green" with His word. Many times children do something out of ignorance they shouldn't have done such as; pick up a dead bird that has fallen from a tree not realizing it may be full of a disease, or wanting to see mom in the hospital so they get in the car of a stranger to get a ride. The outcome of the child is ok, but out of our own fear as parents of the "what if" we get angry with the child leaving them hurt, confused, and fearful instead of loved. Yes, we need to teach them, but teach them in love, not fear.

"Neither any trees; *but only those men which have not the seal of God in their foreheads."* What are these trees? They are humanity. Mark 8:24, *"And he looked up, and said, I see men as trees, walking."* Judges 9:8, *"The trees went forth on a time to anoint a king over them; and they said unto the olive tree, Reign thou over us."*

John has written three illustrations (grass, green things, and trees) to say the same thing; "don't hurt one another with the power that is in the word- the Torah of God, but give them life." Paul tells us in Philippians 4:6-9, *"Be careful for nothing; but in **every thing** by prayer and supplication with **thanksgiving** let your requests be made known unto God. And the **peace of God**, which passeth **all understanding**, shall keep your hearts and minds through Christ Jesus."*

> *"Finally, brethren, whatever things are true, whatever things are noble, whatever things are just, whatever things are pure, whatever things are lovely, whatever things are of good report, if there is any virtue and if there is anything praiseworthy—meditate on these things" (Philippians 4:8).*

If we know God as our heavenly Father, we should know Him and His word as PEACE that passes all our natural understanding. John 20:21, *"Then said Jesus to them again, Peace be unto you: as my Father hath sent me, even so send I you."*

Many times because of our own ignorance when we pray we reflect our insecurities and judgments that cause others to be in bondage instead of setting the captives free as Jesus did. Illustration: Let us suppose we find out someone close to us had an affair. Let's pretend this person has been married for 10-20 years, has a spouse with 2 kids, is very successful with their career, has a good reputation in the community, and they are a Sunday school teacher in the local church. What kind of prayers are going out for this person when the secret of the affair is exposed?

The following is a sample of two different ways to pray for the same thing; one is of a person that sees things with their natural understanding, and the other is from a person who is praying as a son of God:

Dear God,

I am praying for_____. Please God, you know of all this _____, _____, and _____ that is in their life. They know better than to be doing this, and I just do not understand why they keep it up. Their life is just full of_____, _____, and _____. It is really causing me and _____, _____, and _____ so much grief to know they are going through this. God please change them and make them stop hurting themselves and others, including myself. Thanks God. Amen

Notice in the prayer how much negativism there is?

Dear Father,

In the name that is above every name let your identity; your love; and your character be manifested. (Person's name), I hear the word of God, and I know that you are better than that. I know that you are a son of God. I surround you as I pray in the Holy Ghost with words that are words of power and life. I support your godly life. (Person's name), I call you to be a manifestation of who you truly are: to act, think, and talk like Jesus Christ. I declare and decree that people will come from afar to lead, guide, and support you in your true identity, and that you will be opened to receive their love that God has given them to give to you as you move forward and advance with the empowerment of the Holy Spirit. The Spirit of God is resident in you and upon you, and He will break all of those things that are trying to destroy you. In Jesus name let His Life come forth in your life. Amen

"But only those men which have not the seal of God in their foreheads." What is the seal of God? The Holy Spirit reveals to us the mind of Christ that is in us. This is not about whether we are children of God, but whether we are mature in Christ. Many people consider themselves Christians, but translate the word of God with their natural understanding, which brings separation, division, and death. Romans 8:6-8, *"For to be carnally minded is death; but to be spiritually minded is **life and peace**. Because the carnal mind is enmity against God: for it is not subject to the law of God, neither indeed can be. So then they that are in the flesh* (natural understanding) *cannot please God."* Romans 8:13-14, *"For if ye live after the flesh* (natural understanding), *ye shall die: but if ye through the Spirit* (mind of Christ) *do mortify the deeds of the body, ye shall live. For as many as are led by the Spirit of God* (mind of Christ), *they are the **sons of God**."* They are over comers in the body of Christ doing the Father's business as Jesus did, counting no man's sins against him, but cleansing the world of all unrighteousness by seeing the world through the mind of Christ. This is not the wrath of God but the passion of His love that takes us through the journey of being born again cleansing out the old Adam, and preparing our mind and heart to rule with Him in the earth today.

Matthew 18:18-22:

> *"Verily I say unto you, whatsoever ye shall bind on earth shall be bound in heaven: and whatsoever ye shall loose on earth shall be loosed in heaven. Again, I say unto you, that if two of you shall agree on earth as touching any thing that they shall ask, it shall be done for them of my Father, which is in heaven. For where two or three are gathered together in my name, there am I in the midst of them. Then came Peter to him, and said, **Lord, how oft shall my brother sin against me, and I forgive him? Till seven***

times? Jesus saith unto him, I say not unto thee, until seven times: but, until seventy times seven."

Many things in a person's past can bring them to a point of doing something they know they should not do. If we judge them because of what they did yesterday, we miss the opportunity to be a son of God radiating with His love, compassion, and mercy. It does

Jesus had no outward beauty to behold, just as we do not. He gave us His beauty of Christ for our ashes of death.

not nullify the sin, but it does give life for them to move beyond the sin. The laws of reaping and sowing will still take place, but as sons of God, we have the opportunity to help someone be an overcomer when dark situations arise, or we can bring judgment and separation to the body of Christ. This is the wisdom of Revelation verse 4.

Those that have the seal of God, or the mind of Christ, will recall to their remembrance by the Holy Spirit who they were before they were conceived in the womb of their mother (Jeremiah 1:5). Isaiah tells us in 46:9-10, *"Remember the former things of old: for I am God, and there is none else; I am God, and there is none like me, **Declaring the end from the beginning, and from ancient times the things that are not yet done,** saying, My counsel shall stand, and I will do all my pleasure."* Verse 4 is not referring to harming the literal men that do not have the seal of God, but allowing the word of God which is full of love and mercy to destroy the ego of self control leaving them with a desire to want to know their heavenly Father because He first loved them.

Verse 5: *"And to them it was given that they should not kill them, but that they should be tormented five months: and their torment was as the torment of a scorpion, when he striketh a man."*

We just covered most of what this verse is talking about in the previous verse. The five months is symbolic of the number for grace. However, if we are not receiving the grace that is available to us, then what we are going through will seem like tormenting darkness full of pain and bondage.

> *The Lord's Feast are pillars in His calendar to meet with man. There are 5 months between Passover and Rosh Hashanah, or blowing of the trumpets. History reveals complacency in Christ and mixture of the world in the children of God where they are most vulnerable to the tactics of the enemy of God.*

Verse 6: *"And in those days shall men seek death, and shall not find it; and shall desire to die, and death shall flee from them."*

We have all been in situations where we see no hope. The problem is that we usually try to come up with solutions made from our own creation instead of surrendering it all to God and allowing His peace to be in control. When a person is going through a dark place in their life, this "death" referred to in verse 6 may seem like a literal dying of the flesh; but once the bullets of the ego have been fired, and the Spirit of God is in control, the flesh should not need to go through a natural death and the soul will release its control allowing the mind of Christ to lead. Galatians 2:20-21 says, *"I am crucified with Christ: nevertheless I live; yet not I, but Christ liveth in me: and the life which I now live in the flesh I live by the faith of the Son of God, who loved me, and gave himself for me. I do not frustrate the grace of God:"*

God is not glorified by us going through a natural death to come into His presence. He is glorified when we come into His presence as a son of God while in our natural body bringing the unity of faith lifting up the body of Christ as one.

After the scorching summer heat season is over, there is the blowing of the shofar that is heard at Rosh Hashanah. This is the New Year of the civil calendar used to decree when the earth was created, not the Gregorian calendar used today. This is the time for the church, depicted as the ten virgins asleep with the light of God in them, to wake up and trim their wicks for their light to shine bright for the bridegroom is coming. Those that did not have the oil of the Holy Spirit which was given as Pentecost, not Passover, will need to go back and get their own oil (Matthew 25).

Verse 7: *"And the shapes of the locusts were like unto horses prepared unto battle; and on their heads were as it were crowns like gold, and their faces were as the faces of men."*

Remember, the bottomless pit, or our imagination has been let loose and what is coming out of us is the mind-destroying locusts that cause those negative emotions, pain, sorrow, and suffering scribed likened to the sting of a scorpion's tail. In the Bible, horses are symbolic of power. These locusts are fighting the mind of Christ with humanistic

Locusts are one of the few insects that were permitted to eat under the Biblical dietary laws.

strength or natural intellect trying to justify the ways of God to their understanding. Paul tells us in Romans 8:5-8, *"Those who live according to the sinful nature have their minds set on what that nature desires; but those who live in accordance with the Spirit have their minds set on what the Spirit desires. The mind of sinful man is death, but the mind controlled by the Spirit is life and peace; the sinful mind is hostile to God. It does not submit to God's law, nor can it do so. Those controlled by the sinful nature cannot please God"* (NIV).

When we allow the Spirit of God in us to be in control while we rest in His peace telling our mind that we are "new creatures in Christ;" there is no sting of the scorpion and nothing for the locust to devour. A dead man cannot be tormented. In 2 Chronicles 20:15 we read about the Lord telling the king and the people, *"Be not afraid nor dismayed by reason of this great multitude; for the battle is not yours, but*

God's." This "reason" is what our natural understanding is telling our mind making judgmental decisions on our emotions and what we see or hear.

When trials and tribulations come our way, God wants us to trust Him first. Matthew 6:24-7:2 reads:

> *"Therefore I tell you, do not worry about your life, what you will eat or drink; or about your body, what you will wear. Is not life more important than food, and the body more important than clothes? Look at the birds of the air; they do not sow, reap, or store away in barns, and yet your heavenly Father feeds them. Are you not much more valuable than they? Who of you by worrying can add a single hour to his life? And why do you worry about clothes? See how the lilies of the field grow. They do not labor or spin. Yet I tell you that not even Solomon in all his splendor was dressed like one of these. If that is how God clothes the grass of the field, which is here today and tomorrow is thrown into the fire, will he not much more clothe you, O you of little faith? So do not worry, saying, 'What shall we eat?' or 'What shall we drink?' or 'What shall we wear?' For the pagans run after all these things, and your heavenly Father knows that you need them. But seek first his kingdom and his righteousness, and all these things will be given to you as well. Therefore do not worry about tomorrow, for tomorrow will worry about itself. Each day has enough trouble of its own. Do not judge, or you too will be judged. For in the same way you judge others, you will be judged, and with the measure you use, it will be measured to you"* (NIV).

On the heads of these locusts are crowns LIKE gold. Gold speaks of the character and nature of God. These people profess Christianity, but use human reason to interpret the word of God causing separation and division to the body of Christ. John clarifies their identity when he writes, "their faces were as the faces of men." In many churches today, we have lessons in psychology coming from the pulpit where the leadership is using the word of God to justify right and wrong instead of allowing the Holy Spirit to reveal our heavenly Father's love.

Much of the church understands the Passover season and resurrection of Christ Jesus. Some even realize the Feast of Pentecost and the connection with the filling of the Holy Spirit. However, the majority of the church of Jesus Christ honors Him at Christmas as a baby in a manger, then puts Him on a cross at Passover with a lukewarm season until Christmas comes around again and He is back in a manger. The in between season from Passover to the next Christmas are filled with Biblical journeys that God established for mankind to meet with Him. These established feast days of God are our growth and development markers as new creations in Christ to climb mount Zion bringing His Kingdom into the earth today.

Verse 8: *"And they had hair as the hair of women, and their teeth were as the teeth of lions."*

This verse is not talking about literal women, but the soul of humankind being in control of the temple of God or body of Christ. The lion is known as the king of beasts, not sons of God. The teeth represent what is being chewed and digested going into the body. All of this is symbolic of Christians taking in the word of God while using their natural understanding to discern what Scripture is saying. Remember

Hair carries the DNA identity of humanity, yet it is a dead matter used to protect the covering of the flesh.

Romans 8:5-6 says. *"Those who live according to the sinful nature have their minds set on what that nature desires; but those who live in accordance with the Spirit have their minds set on what the Spirit desires. The mind of sinful man is death, but the mind controlled by the Spirit is life and peace"* (NIV).

Verse 9: *"And they had breastplates, as it were breastplates of iron; and the sound of their wings was as the sound of chariots of many horses running to battle."*

John is describing the Hellenism doctrine of the scriptures that has entered into the heart of the church. Today if we ask what Paul is seeing with his description of the armor of God found in Ephesians 6 we would say he is describing a Roman soldier. This is a Hellenistic or Greek thought, but the truth is Paul is teaching as a Rabbi describing the garments of the High Priest.

Where does a person wear a breastplate? It is worn over the heart. This is where God planted His identity in each of us (Eccl. 3:11). Iron speaks of the hardness of the shield we have placed over the heart, which keeps His identity from being released. This "iron" is filled with "justification" and "self" concern. Psalms 81:11-13, *"But my people* (Christians) *would not hearken to my voice; and Israel* (body of Christ, the 10 lost tribes) *would none of me. So I gave them up unto their own hearts' lust* (natural understanding that brings death)*: and they walked in their own counsels. Oh that my people had hearkened unto me, and Israel had walked in my ways!"*

The word "wings" should be connected with healing. On the four corners of a Hebrew prayer shawl there are long strands known as Tzitzits. They are known as "wings." This is what the woman with the blood issue touched of Jesus and she was healed.

The "wings" symbolize movement, and the "chariots" symbolize the vessel carrying the word of God. The "horses" symbolize the aggression that is taking place in the body of Christ when led by the soul of humankind instead of the Spirit of God. In 2 Chronicles 20:15 we are told, *"Thus saith the LORD unto you, be not afraid nor dismayed by reason of this great multitude; for the battle is not yours, but God's."* The horses should be the dunamis power of grace given by the Holy Spirit within the word we release over the situation.

As sons of God following Jesus with the mind of Christ, our battles must be fought from Mt. Zion by the Holy Spirit, or the inner court where the mercy seat of God is.

Many Christians go into battle from the middle court of the Tabernacle. Scripture refers to this as Mt. Moriah where the "sand" company of Abraham's family dwells. The heart will say one thing, but the mind will justify another causing mixture and emotional turmoil. Decisions need to be made, yet making those decisions from faith versus fear becomes an inner battle on how to move forward.

A large majority of Christians try to fight battles for God from the outer court known as the hill of Ophel where the "dust" company focuses their Christian relationship with God. In 1 John these two realms are discussed as "little children" and "young men." John however talked to the father, which shows he had the mind of an over-comer sitting at the right hand of God. Abraham was told this would be the "star" company that sees life from the heavens instead of the earth.

Let us read what David has to say about his soul being among the lions in Psalms 57:1-11:

> *"Be merciful unto me, O God, be merciful unto me: for my **soul** trusteth in thee: yea, in the shadow of **thy wings** (movements, ways) will I make my refuge (trust and rest), until these calamities (battles) be overpast. I will cry unto God most high; unto God that performeth (the battle is the Lord's) **all things** for me. He shall **send from heaven** (His understanding and ways from our heart), and save from the reproach of him (soul control) that would swallow me up. Selah. **God shall send forth** his mercy and his truth (inner court understanding). **My soul is among lions** (religious Christians): and I lie even among them that are **set on fire** (using the word*

of God for justification to destroy), *even the **sons of men*** (allowing the soul to be in control of the body of Christ), *whose **teeth are spears and arrows, and their tongue a sharp sword*** (where God's word is being released). *Be thou exalted, O God, above the heavens; **let thy glory be above all the earth*** (the glory of God is His sons that minister to the body of Christ as Jesus did). *They* (religious minds) *have prepared a net* (trying to justify God) *for my steps; my soul is bowed down: they have **digged a pit*** (imagination) *before me, into the midst whereof **they are fallen themselves*** (create our own destruction with our imagination). *Selah. My heart is fixed, O God, my heart is fixed: **I will sing and give praise*** (the Alter of Incense is before the mercy seat of God). *Awake up, my glory; awake, psaltery and harp: I myself will awake early. I will praise thee, O Lord, among the people: I will sing unto thee among the nations. For thy mercy is great unto the heavens, and thy truth unto the clouds. Be thou exalted, O God, above the heavens: let thy glory be above all the earth.*"

Verse 10: *"And they had tails like unto scorpions, and there were stings in their tails: and their power was to hurt men five months."*

These tails are the false prophets, or people that take the word of God to bring justification and condemnation to the body of Christ (Isaiah 9:15-16). The "sting" is the intimidation that comes upon the body stirring the soul of man to dwell in their heart and mind upon doom and gloom, or fear and anxiety instead of giving praises to God that He is in control.

Proverbs 30:4-5:
"Who has established all the ends of the earth?
What is his name, and the name of his son?
Tell me if you know!

Every word of God is flawless;
he is a shield to those who take refuge in him" (NIV).

The number "five" is the number of grace when used according to the mind of Christ. However; if it is used by taking the word of God to justify good and evil, it becomes the number of death and destruction. This verse is not talking about a literal time, but illustrates what happens when people try to use the word of God for justification. The Tree of Knowledge of Good and Evil never gave humankind the Life of God. Jesus was crucified on this tree, and it is not meant to come back again. Unfortunately, humanity has allowed "ego" back into the picture, which gives place to that which is antichrist. Let us read the following conversation that Jesus had with those that considered themselves the children of God in John 8:36-45:

> *"If the Son therefore shall make you free, ye shall be free indeed. I know that ye are Abraham's seed; but ye seek to kill me, because my word hath no place in you. I speak that which I have seen with my Father* (God)*: and ye do that which ye have seen with your father* (ego)*. They answered and said unto him, Abraham is our father. Jesus saith unto them, if ye were Abraham's children, ye would do the works of Abraham* (live by faith in God)*. But now ye seek to kill me, a* **man** *that hath told you the truth, which I have heard of God: this did not Abraham. Ye do the deeds of your father* (natural understanding)*. Then said they to him, we be not born of fornication* (this is explained in Romans 7)*; we have one Father, even God. Jesus said unto them, If God were your Father, ye would love me* (Deut. 10:19)*: for I proceeded forth and came from God; neither came I of myself, but he sent me. Why do ye not understand my speech? Even because ye cannot hear my word,* (they had a breastplate of iron around their heart)*. Ye are of your father the devil* (ego, self)*, and the lusts of your father ye will do. He* (first Adam)

was a murderer from the beginning, and abode not in the truth, because there is no truth in him. When he speaketh a lie (changing the character and nature of God's word), *he speaketh of his own: for he is a liar, and the father of it. And because I tell you the truth, ye believe me not."*

Verse 11: *"And they had a king over them, which is the angel of the bottomless pit, whose name in the Hebrew tongue is Abaddon, but in the Greek tongue hath his name Apollyon."*

Many of the words in the verse we have already talked about, but to help us understand let us review. The word "king" represents someone given power and authority. Rev. 1:6 told us that Jesus Christ made us kings and priests unto God.

Remember, the word "angel" means "messenger." This would be someone that has been given a word from the Lord to share with the body of Christ to edify and unite the body. This might be someone of the five-fold ministry: a pastor, prophet, teacher, an evangelist, or apostle. It may be someone that is just following the unction of the Holy Spirit. However, this messenger functions by the imagination of carnal understanding (symbolized by the bottomless pit) versus the mind of Christ. In Psalms 28:1, David cries out to God to keep him from allowing his imagination to take control, *"Unto thee will I cry, O LORD my rock; be not silent to me: lest, if thou be silent to me, I become like them that go down into the pit."*

The name "Abaddon" in Hebrew and the name "Apollyon" in Greek mean the same thing: The destroyer, exterminator. Paul uses this word when talking to a body of believers in 1 Corinthians 10:10, *"Neither murmur ye, as some of them also murmured, and were destroyed of the destroyer."* He gives the illustration in the previous verses about the children of Israel being saved and baptized with Moses, but they tried to tempt Christ with their murmuring and complaining. We have the mind of Christ today. When our body and soul are going through trials, we are not supposed to challenge the Spirit of God in us with doubt and complaining, but live by faith believing *"that all things work together for good to them that love God, to them who are the called according to his purpose"* (Romans 8:28).

Verse 11 is not referring to one person being raised up as the "antichrist." We are each a "king" of the soul and body that we are in. By the words of our mouth, we can create life, or we can create death to ourselves, and those that are connected to the territory we live in. Proverbs 20:8AMP, *"A [discerning] king who sits on the throne of judgment sifts all evil [like chaff] with his eyes [and cannot be easily fooled]."* In Matthew 7:1-2 we read, *"Do not judge, or you too will be judged. For in the same way you judge others, you will be judged, and with the measure you use, it will be measured to you"* (NIV).

Peter shares with us how we should be with one another in 1 Peter 5:2-14. In these verses, he is talking to Christians. The usage of the words "adversary the devil" in verse 8 is referring to our natural understanding that will try to cause separation and division in the body of Christ by subtly allowing "ego" to enter into the understanding of God's word. *"Every kingdom divided against itself is brought to desolation, and every city or house divided against itself will not stand"* (Matthew 12:25).

> *"Feed the flock of God which is among you, taking the oversight thereof, not by constraint, but willingly; not for filthy lucre, but of a ready mind; Neither as being lords over God's heritage, but being **examples to the flock.** And when the chief Shepherd shall appear, ye shall receive a crown of glory that fadeth not away. Likewise, ye younger, submit yourselves unto the elder. Yea, all of you be subject one to another, and be clothed with humility: for God resisteth the proud, and giveth grace to the humble. Humble yourselves therefore under the mighty hand of God, that he may exalt you in due time: Casting all your*

care upon him; for he careth for you. **Be sober, be vigilant; because your adversary the devil (ego), as a roaring lion, walketh about, seeking whom he may devour:** *Whom resist steadfast in the faith, knowing that the same afflictions are accomplished in your brethren that are in the world. But the God of all grace, who hath called us unto his eternal glory by Christ Jesus, after that ye have suffered a while, make you perfect, stablish, strengthen, settle you. To him be glory and dominion forever and ever. Amen. By Silvanus, a faithful brother unto you, as I suppose, I have written briefly, exhorting, and testifying that* **this is the true grace of God wherein ye stand.** *The church that is at Babylon, elected together with you, saluteth you; and so doth Marcus my son.* **Greet ye one another with a kiss of charity.** *Peace be with you all that are in Christ Jesus. Amen."*

Verse 12: *"One woe is past; and, behold, there come two woes more hereafter."*

Remember what these "woes" are? Woe, woe, woe equals pain, grief, and suffering. As long as we stay in the outer or middle court mentality, we are "serpent's food" or mixing our Christian life with our carnal understanding. Again, all of the courts in the temple represent the body of Christ, but there is a different relationship experience with the Father depending on which court one dwells in: Outer court – saved by grace, but retaining a slave mentality. Middle court – knowing one is a child of God, but having various levels of growth and development from child level to sonship doing the Father's business. Inner court – knowing one is a bride of Christ desiring to have oneness spirit, soul, and body with the Beloved Jesus Christ. We say we trust God and have faith in Him, but we mix that faith with our senses and justification. Those that come boldly to the throne of God cannot take anything of "ego" into the Holy of Holies. Only God can be in there. Selah.

What happened when serpents were biting the children of Israel? Let us read

Numbers 21:6-9:

"And the LORD sent fiery serpents among the people, and they bit the people; and much people of Israel died. Therefore, the people came to Moses, and said, we have sinned, for we have spoken against the LORD, and against thee; pray unto the LORD, that he take away the serpents from us. And Moses prayed for the people. And the LORD said unto Moses, Make thee a fiery serpent, and set it upon a pole: and it shall come to pass, that every one that is bitten, when he looketh upon it, shall live. And Moses made a serpent of brass, and put it upon a pole, and it came to pass, that if a serpent had bitten any man, when he beheld the serpent of brass, he lived."

What are these "fiery serpents?" They are the words of their mouth that were causing their own death (Matthew 7:2). The brass is symbolic of human understanding. The "pole" is a "tree." This is a picture of Jesus becoming the curse and hanging on the Tree of Knowledge of Good and Evil to do away with all sin. *"Seek ye first the kingdom of God, and his righteousness; and all these things shall be added unto you"* (Matthew 6:33). We were once enslaved to sin, but the life we now live is unto Christ. We do not have to dodge the snakes, but come up to our heavenly identity in Him where snakes and lions cannot roam.

We have the keys to the kingdom of heaven and the depth of hell, or bottomless pit, will not prevail unless we give place to it. The rock of revelation knowledge that Peter revealed in Matthew 16:16-19 is the rock we too must stand on. Once we establish who Jesus Christ is, then we must establish who we are. *"As He is, so are we in this world"* (1 John 4:17).

Verse 13: *"And the sixth angel sounded, and I heard a voice from the four horns of the golden altar which is before God,"*

The number six is the number of humankind. This verse is declaring that humanity is sounding a message for the world to hear. The number four speaks of completeness; the four corners of the world; ALL. The horns speak of authority. Golden is the character and nature of God. A message is going out for all humankind around the world to hear sounded from the Christ identity within individual people. What is this message? The blowing of the Ram's horn; our jubilee is now here; it is finished; let the glory (sonship) of the Lord fill the earth with transformation of the bride who has made herself ready to consummate the marriage of the LAMB.

Verse 14: *"Saying to the sixth angel which had the trumpet, Loose the four angels which are bound in the great river Euphrates."*

Again, the number four means completeness or the four corners of the earth. The great river Euphrates is symbolic of the power found in water. This river is in Egypt, which is symbolic of the world system. Have you ever seen a powerful waterfall like Niagara Falls? It is breathtaking to see such beauty and energy in God's creation, but if one is not careful and goes over the falls, the power and force could cause instant death.

Passover – desert/ wilderness experience Pentecost – fire experience Tabernacles – water experience. Out of our belly will flow rivers of living water circumcised by the heart of love and out of our mouth our hearts will speak.

Water represents the word of God. When we have His word in us, we have His power and authority. Unfortunately, many of us have minds likened to the Assyrian or the Samaritan where their spiritual mind mixes with the natural creating death instead of life. Proverbs 18:21, *"Death and life are in the power of the tongue: and they that love it shall eat the fruit thereof."* God is Spirit. His kingdom must be all Spirit. We have the ability to come into His presence in the Holy of Holies, but we cannot bring anything of "self" or "ego" to the throne of God. God can only fellowship with His character and image.

Verse 15: *"And the four angels were loosed, which were prepared for an hour, and a day, and a month, and a year, for to slay the third part of men."*

This verse can bring fear and judgment if we are not reading and understanding with the mind of Christ. Remember, the angels are messengers (people) around the world to declare at different seasons and times, our real identity is found in Christ. Paul writes in Colossians 1:26-28, *"Even the mystery which hath been hid from ages and from generations, but now is made manifest to his saints: To whom God would make known what is the riches of the glory of this mystery among the Gentiles; which is Christ in you, the hope of glory: Whom we preach, warning every man, and teaching every man in all wisdom; that we may present every man perfect in Christ Jesus."*

The slaying of a third part of men is not literally killing people, but removing the outer court of the tabernacle of God where sin offerings were given for purification of the people. Scripture confirms this in Hebrews 10:7-18 where we read:

> *"Then said I, Lo, I come (in the volume of the book it is written of me,) to do thy will, O God. Above when he said, Sacrifice and offering and burnt offerings and offering for sin thou wouldest not, neither hadst pleasure therein; which are offered by the law; Then said he, Lo, I come to do thy will, O God.* **He taketh away the first that he may establish the second. By the which will we are sanctified through the offering of the body of Jesus Christ once for all.** *And every priest standeth daily ministering and offering oftentimes the same sacrifices, which can never take away sins: But this man, after he had offered one sacrifice for sins for ever, sat down on the right hand of God; From henceforth expecting till his*

enemies be made his footstool. For by one offering he hath perfected forever them that are sanctified. Whereof the Holy Ghost also is a witness to us: for after that he had said before, this is the covenant that I will make with them after those days, saith the Lord, I will put my laws into their hearts, and in their minds will I write them; And their sins and iniquities will I remember no more. Now where remission of these is, there is no more offering for sin"

Jesus took the outer court sacrifice system away over 2000 years ago. In the eyes of God, there is no saved or unsaved, Jew or Gentile. Jesus paid the total BRIDE price for the sin offering that justified death to mankind for missing the mark of God's teachings. The message of the "angels" is clarified by Paul when he writes to Timothy, *"Be not thou therefore ashamed of the testimony of our Lord, nor of me his prisoner: but be thou partaker of the afflictions of the gospel **according to the power of God; Who hath saved us**, and called us with an holy calling, not according to our works, but according to his own purpose and grace, which was **given us in Christ Jesus before the world began,** But is now made manifest by the appearing of our Savior Jesus Christ, who **hath abolished death, and hath brought life and immortality to light through the gospel:** Whereunto I am appointed a preacher, and an apostle, and a teacher* (angel) *of the Gentiles"* (2 Timothy 1:8-11).

Verse 16: *"And the number of the army of the horsemen were two hundred thousand thousand: and I heard the number of them."*

The army of the "horsemen" is not a literal army, but the "self-ego" that interprets the word of God for justifying instead of cleansing and edifying. The number used in this verse is not an actual number, but the word "myriads" which means "innumerable amounts."

Verse 17: *"And thus I saw the horses in the vision, and them that sat on them, having breastplates of fire, and of jacinth, and brimstone: and the* *heads of the horses were as the heads of lions; and out of their mouths issued fire and smoke and brimstone."*

Remember we have a picture of messengers of God being released around the world declaring a trumpet cry that our Jubilee is today. There is nothing more for Jesus to do that was not completed at Calvary. It is up to us to recognize and believe that today we are new creatures in Christ and as He is so are we in this world. When this message is declared, who do you think will be the first to oppose it? It will be the religious system we call the church because the control they have on the people (calling it doctrine and theology) will be challenged. With it will also be the money system of the church controlling the tithe and storehouse of God. Jesus was confronted with the same issues.

The breastplates symbolize what covers the heart of religion or the people in control of the church. Fire represents purification. Jacinth is a stone that changes color likened to a chameleon that changes to blend in with the environment. Many messengers of God are teaching the Scriptures according to what the people want to hear instead of being led by the Holy Spirit. Brimstone is sulfur that was used through out the Old Testament in the sacrifices for purification. The fire and brimstone purifies and corrects. It does not seem like there would be anything wrong with that except this purification is done with fear and control instead of the love of the Father.

The heads of the horses as the heads of lions is symbolic as well. A lion in Scripture could refer to Jesus as the Lion of the tribe of Judah; or as our adversary, the devil, walking around as a roaring lion seeking whom he may devour. This symbolic lion is in opposition to the messengers of God. Again, these are people that know the word of God, but rather than edifying and encouraging one another in love to bring unity to the body of Christ; they use the word of God to bring fear, separation, and division scaring people to become Christians.

A tool to use in considering which lion is speaking, remember the conversation which took place at Calvary between Jesus and the two thieves. There was a "lion's voice" coming from the thief of the past on one side of Jesus and a "lion's voice" from the thief of the future on His other side. Both voices were releasing the sound of the accuser of the brethren: "If you are, then do...when you get to where you're going, remember me"

Verse 18: *"By these three was the third part of men killed, by the fire, and by the smoke, and by the brimstone, which issued out of their mouths."*

The three elements: fire, smoke, and brimstone are coming from the mouths of the horses with lion's heads. If this were literal, this would be a gruesome picture of a "fire breathing beast." However, these beasts are really those that speak the word of God to bring judgment and condemnation to the body of Christ. Again, fire and brimstone are for purification. Smoke is symbolic of ignorance, darkness, and cloudiness. The person using the word of God does not see clearly and is bringing death to those in the outer court that are seeking mercy.

> *When we try to make decisions looking into muddy waters, we do not see the hazards, depths, or clarity that may be lie waiting in the deep. This is when either fear or faith determines our move.*

Verse 19: *"For their power is in their mouth, and in their tails: for their tails were like unto serpents, and had heads, and with them they do hurt."*

If we took these Scriptures literally, we would now have a horse with a lion's head sending fire, brimstone, and smoke out of its mouth with a tail of a snake. Talk about our imagination going wild! This sounds like a horrible Halloween costume. Yet, the reality is how far many Christians go to distort the truth and love of God's word. I have been around these people and felt the persecution of their mouth. *"Death and life are in the power of the tongue: and they that love it shall eat the fruit thereof"* (Proverbs 18:21). *"Judge not, that ye be not judged. For with what judgment ye judge, ye shall be judged: and with what measure ye mete, it shall be measured to you again"* (Matthew 7:1-2).

> *The sting of the tail is symbolic of what we leave behind in the shadow. Did we leave the sweet fragrance of the Holy Spirit, or the smell of fear and death?*

The prophet Isaiah speaks of those whom John is describing. In Chapter 9:15-16 we read, *"The ancient and honourable, he is the head; and the prophet that teacheth lies, he is the tail. For the leaders of this people cause them to err; and they that are led of them are destroyed."* Isaiah shares with us that these people have the word of God in their mind, but what comes out is the equivalent to being a false prophet. The leaders or those sharing their knowledge of God's word are not leading by the Holy Spirit manifesting His peace, love, and truth of His word.

Verse 20: *"And the rest of the men which were not killed by these plagues yet repented not of the works of their hands, that they should not worship devils, and idols of gold, and silver, and brass, and stone, and of wood: which neither can see, nor hear, nor walk:"*

The rest of the men refer to Christians that were so set on their ways of understanding Scripture that they refused to change. This is why we have so many denominations interpreting the word of God not discerning the Lord's body, but teaching with separation and division among the body. Look in any phone book and you will see numerous listings of different churches that all declare to be Christian, but will not have anything to do with one another, even if they are right across the street.

Many in leadership are leading by drawing a crowd with entertainment to increase their following for job security and paycheck. They say they are being led by the Holy Spirit, but if the paycheck were removed, many would be doing another job besides ministry.

Breaking down some of the words in this verse: "devils" refers to an antichrist spirit or using the word of God to justify self-understanding. "Idols" speak of an imagination that exalts itself against God. We have taken the word and character of God (gold) and brought wrath and condemnation instead of love. The gold speaks of an image that we "think" is God. Silver speaks of redemption, but it is not God's redemption for humanity. It is the interpretation of religion. Brass is symbolic of the suffering Jesus went through that we think we understand, but we only have an understanding of what we have created in our own mind. Stone speaks of foundation. Our foundation should be Jesus Christ with each of us having the mind of Christ. Unfortunately, what should be the mind of Christ in us is really a mixture of what we "think." Wood speaks of humanity. Even in this area, we each have only a portion of what humanity is to God.

None of the images that we have created has life in them. They are just our opinion of our understanding. There is nothing wrong for us to receive our portion of what the Holy Spirit reveals. The problem comes when we camp on that revelation and make a religion out of it trying to convince others that we have the whole picture. The body of Christ is made of many members, but is one body. We are supposed to join the body together in love having a teachable Spirit to acknowledge what God is showing others as well. The Apostle Paul tells us that we are not all supposed to be an arm or a leg, but we are to be one body. We need to be re-united. This is the discerning of the Lord's body that we are supposed to understand when taking the Lord's meal.

In John 1:12 we are told that if we receive Him, even His name, that we would be given His power to become the sons of God. Sons of God are peacemakers (Matt. 5:9). They are not necessarily right in their own eyes, but are led by the Holy Spirit with the peace that surpasses understanding everywhere their natural mind does not comprehend logic or reason.

WE must have ears to hear what the Spirit of God is saying. If you believe He is speaking through someone then go to the Scriptures and find the witness of what they are saying, making sure that it lines up with the character and nature of God who is LOVE, LIFE, and LIGHT. In HIM, there is no darkness. It is Christ in you that desire to speak out transforming you into HIS IMAGE to bring unity to HIS BODY.

I've mentioned earlier, the Hellenistic teaching method is to have leadership and pupils – leadership controls and pupils listen and obey without their own thoughts. The Hebrew way is to allow every member of the body of Christ to share their wisdom as a Divine/gold nugget to be the key for someone else's closed door.

Verse 21: *"Neither repented they of their murders, nor of their sorceries, nor of their fornication, nor of their thefts."*

Let us discern some of these words in this verse. "Repent" means to change our way of thinking. What do we need to change about how we think? "Murders" refers to death. Scripture tells us the power of death is in our tongue. What comes out of our mouth begins in our heart. We cause death and destruction by taking the word of God and bringing judgment, condemnation, and separation to the body of Christ. This is not the mind of Christ that Jesus gave us.

The word "sorceries" is the same as word witchcraft. For us today it is the word "Pharmacia." Now we are not implying that it is wrong to take medicine. This verse is talking spiritual. What do medicines do to the body? They alter the mind. This is what the word "sorceries" is implying to the body of Christ. Instead of sharing the word of God with the mind of Christ, there are those that alter the understanding of Scripture to justify and condemn. This is a spirit of deviation taking what God calls good from the Tree of Life, and conforming it into good on the Tree of Knowledge that leads to death via justification.

The word "fornication" is not a literal sexual relationship outside of marriage, but the body of Christ listening and living a life that is not with the mind of Christ. The fornication is against Jesus. Paul shares in Romans chapter 7 of the woman that was married to her first husband – Adam who is now dead. She is legally qualified to marry again which she does with Jesus Christ taking the name of her new husband, but when she tries to have intimacy with her husband Jesus Christ, she keeps remembering her husband Adam who died. Selah.

The word "thefts" takes us to the Scriptures in John 10:8-10, *"All that ever came before me* (representing God) *are thieves and robbers: but the sheep did not hear them. I am the door: by me if any man enter in, he shall be saved, and shall go in and out, and find pasture. The thief cometh not, but for to steal, and to kill, and to destroy* (by their tongues)*: I am* (TRUTH, THE WORD of GOD) *come that they might* (it is already our inheritance since Calvary) *have life* (resurrection of immortality), *and that they might have it more abundantly."*

Believing that Jesus Christ is our personal Savior is our Passover experience coming from death to LIFE. We must then journey into our wilderness to grow up in Christ which is Pentecost. With our identity in Him and the teachings of the Holy Spirit we prepare ourselves to be the bride our bridegroom is coming to consummate His marriage with His church.

In Romans 8:29 Paul says, *"For whom he did foreknow, he also did predestinate to be conformed to the image of his Son, that he might be the firstborn among many brethren."* The words "to be" are not part of the original. King James added them. When we take those words out the verse reads that we are today made in HIS image, the image of Jesus Christ. It is not something that we have to work at or do, but it is the faith of God in us, which will bring forth this revelation of our true identity. We will no longer wonder who we really are, or question if God still loves us if we do something wrong. We are not going to be created; we already are in His image.

Proverbs 14:12, *"There is a way which seemeth right unto a man, but the end thereof are the ways of death."*

Romans 8:5-8, *"For they that are after the flesh do mind the things of the flesh; but they that are after the Spirit the things of the Spirit. For to be carnally minded is death; but to be spiritually minded is life and peace. Because the carnal mind is enmity against God: for it is not subject to the law of God, neither indeed can be. So then they that are in the flesh cannot please God."*

Paul tells us that we must put off our old way of thinking and be new creatures in Christ (2 Corinthians 5:17). Today, we are a new humanity infused with the Spirit of God. The book of Revelation has been written to reveal Christ in each of us first individually, then corporately to bring unity to one body so that Christ will be manifested all and in ALL.

Colossians 3:9-17:

> *"Lie not one to another, seeing that ye have put off the old man with his deeds; And have put on the new man, which is renewed in knowledge after the image of him that created him: Where there is neither Greek nor Jew, circumcision nor uncircumcision, Barbarian, Scythian, bond nor free: but Christ is all, and in all. Put on therefore, as the elect of God, holy and beloved, bowels of mercies, kindness, humbleness of mind, meekness, longsuffering; Forbearing one another, and forgiving one another, if any man have a quarrel against any: even as Christ forgave you, so also do ye. And above all these things put on charity, which is*

the bond of perfectness. And let the peace of God rule in your hearts, to the which also ye are called in one body; and be ye thankful. Let the word of Christ dwell in you richly in all wisdom; teaching and admonishing one another in psalms and hymns and spiritual songs, singing with grace in your hearts to the Lord. And whatsoever ye do in word or deed, do all in the name of the Lord Jesus, giving thanks to God and the Father by him."

Notes of Reflection

What were your immediate thoughts in this chapter?

_____

_____

_____

_____

_____

What preconceived thoughts did you have before reading this chapter?

_____

_____

_____

_____

_____

What new information did you learn?

_____

_____

_____

_____

_____

Does this information seem confusing or liberating? Why?

_____

_____

_____

_____

_____

CHAPTER 10

A Strong Angel

"And I saw another mighty angel come down from heaven, clothed with a cloud: and a rainbow was upon his head, and his face was as it were the sun, and his feet as pillars of fire:"

Leaving chapter nine we put six angels behind us to open chapter ten with number seven. Remember that an "angel" is a messenger, not necessarily a winged creature flying around. The number of each messenger is connected to the growth and development of our coming into the understanding of Christ in us. John uses Old Testament symbolism to describe the process of what our body, soul, and spirit go through to be transformed from children of God into His sons. He is writing from an understanding of the cultural traditions of the Hebrew faith found in the Old Testament. His position is unveiling the wisdom of the Tanakh from a position of the Father's love and not law. Eighty-five percent of the New Testament is drawn from the Old Testament.

The true spirit of prophecy is a message lifting up Jesus Christ; not just one of predicting the future. The Old Testament told us of a coming King. The New Testament tells us that the King has come and is uniting His Kingdom to rule and reign with Him today as the Kingdom of Heaven in the earth.

Each of the chapters in Revelation builds upon one another. We take key words that John wrote and use the Scriptures to see how they were used.

Verse 1: *"another mighty angel"* would be the seventh messenger. The number seven in Scripture is the number of completion. It refers to resting in God. We cannot rest in God if our mind is not at peace. It does not mean that there is peace around us, but peace within us. This resting place requires more than an individual relationship with God. We cannot have "peace that surpasses our understanding" just for ourselves. We may justify to ourselves that this is the peace of God, but it is not. To come into rest with God, we must see the **corporate realm**. This "mighty angel" is the Christ who is one body.

Jesus Christ is the head of a many member body, but it is still only one body. Let us consider our natural body as an illustration: If some portion of our natural flesh is hurting, can the rest of the body declare 100% wellness? Of course not! If you stubbed your toe and said, "I'm doing great" that toe would start to let you know that you are not doing so great and will force you to hobble because of its pain.

The same thing goes with the corporate body of Christ. If we are seeing ourselves as "sons of God" but looking upon another person as a "sinner saved by grace" we are not yet truly qualified to do the Father's business.

This corporate body, or seventh angel, is coming down from heaven. So our next question would be where is heaven? Scripture does not tell us it is out in space somewhere; but where God is:

- **Luke 17:20-21,** *"And when he was demanded of the Pharisees, when the kingdom of God should come, he answered them and said, The kingdom of God cometh not with observation: Neither shall they say, Lo here! Or, lo there! For, behold, **the kingdom of God is within you.**"*

- **Romans 14:17,** *"For the kingdom of God is not meat and drink; but righteousness, and peace, and joy in the Holy Ghost."*

- **1 Corinthians 4:20-21,** *"For the kingdom of God is not in word, but in power* (unconditional love.) *What will ye? Shall I come unto you with a rod, or in love, and in the spirit of meekness?"*

The corporate body of Christ is "descending" or manifesting individually the revelation of Jesus Christ as the Holy Spirit reveals to them that it is Christ in them. This is not going to be some kind of an array of fire works displayed in the sky that we are supposed to watch with people riding on white horses following Jesus as he carries a flaming sword and does hurdles from one cloud to another. We might see this image on the movie screen, but John is not talking about movies. The word "descend" is not literally "coming out of the sky," but coming out from within ourselves. A son of God is one who has experienced the mercy seat of God, and now has mercy to give away to others.

The cloud is symbolic of the Spirit of God. The corporate body of Christ being manifested on the earth will be clothed with the Holy Spirit. Again, this is not literal white linen floating around in the sky or a literal cloud, which happens to descend on someone transforming their image. **The Spirit of God is within us,** but many people are so self oriented that His Spirit is veiled from revealing the fullness of the Father's glory we each already possess.

The rainbow upon the angel's head tells us that this corporate man is in covenant with God. This revelation builds upon the verses found in chapters 4:3 and 6:2 where the sons of God understood the message of the throne of God. This would be *First fruits are those that are drawn to the Father's teachings and instructions found in the Torah with passion and love for all that the Father desires to release in them while in their natural body.*

different from the perception of those in the body of Christ that have a relationship with God from an outer or middle court experience. These are "first fruits" or "star company people" whose lives are reflecting the mind of Christ.

Paul teaches us this message in 1 Corinthians 2:12-16, *"Now we have received, not the spirit of the world, but the spirit which is of God; that we might know the things that are freely given to us of God. Which things also we speak, not in the words which man's wisdom teacheth, but which the Holy Ghost teacheth; comparing spiritual things with spiritual. But the natural man receiveth not the things of the Spirit of God: for they are foolishness unto him: neither can he know them, because they are spiritually discerned. But he that is spiritual judgeth all things, yet he himself is judged of no man. For who hath known the mind of the Lord, that he may instruct him? **But we have the mind of Christ.**"*

This covenant was made between God and all men before the foundations of the world. God sealed it within each of our hearts and will release the revelation of this understanding to His glory; not ours. Each one of us has a different portion of the glory of God. No one person has all the glory, but each person must release his portion of glory that God gave to bring unity to the body of Christ. The glory of Christ shines through us when the Holy Spirit leads us in the Father's love.

The corporate body of Christ is designed to individually reflect the raiment of Jesus Christ, the son of God. This is the "face that was as the sun" John tells us about that will radiate with light and warmth as the natural sun. When others see a son of God they should see their Heavenly Father; not the individual.

Pillars describe a connection to the foundation (Jesus Christ) with the rest of the temple (body of Christ). These people support, encourage, intercede, and love one another unconditionally so that others can move in the call that God has given them for their life. The strength for "pillars" comes directly from their relationship with God. They know Him with the intimacy of His love, mercy, and grace even while going through personal trials and turmoil.

Pillars have to be tested to make sure they can carry the weight for others who are not as strong. These people have gone through trials making choices to ascend into an intimacy with God instead of settling in the bottomless pit of their imagination. They now have power and authority to be a parent (descending) to others. John's choice of using the word "pillar" allows us to be teachable to more than just one pillar of the body such as; the neck, raised arms, legs, feet, shoulders, and spine. Each of these body parts contains significant spirit wisdom we could reflect upon to encourage and support the body.

The "feet as pillars of fire" are symbolic of the Holy Spirit's anointing affecting the places that we travel. They are the means of supporting and transporting the body that carry each of us through our lifestyles. They are also discussed in the foot washing account found in John 13. Jesus washed the feet of the disciples preparing them for the fullness of the call upon their lives to be sons of God.

"So after he had washed their feet, and had taken his garments, and was set down again, he said unto them, Know ye what I have done to you? Ye call me Master and Lord: and ye say well; for so I am. If I then, your Lord and Master, have washed your feet; ye also ought to wash one another's feet. For I have given you an example, that ye should do as I have done to you. Verily, verily, I say unto you, the servant is not greater than his lord; neither he that is sent greater than he that sent him" (John 13:12-16).

Pillars are the picture of "Jacob's ladder" in Genesis where he dreams of angels ascending and descending connecting heaven and earth.

"And he dreamed, and behold a ladder set up on the earth, and the top of it reached to heaven: and behold the angels

*of God ascending and descending on it. And, behold, the LORD stood above it, and said, I am the LORD God of Abraham thy father, and the God of Isaac: the land whereon thou liest, to thee will I give it, and to thy seed; And thy seed shall be as the dust of the earth, and thou shall spread abroad to the west, and to the east, and to the north, and to the south: and in thee and **in thy seed shall all the families of the earth be blessed.** And, behold, I am with thee, and will keep thee in all places whither thou goes, and will bring thee again into this land; for I will not leave thee, until I have done that which I have spoken to thee of "* (Genesis 28:12-15).

(Oh by the way: notice that God said, "All the families of the earth would be blessed through Jacob" This is one of those places where we have to do a double check about our Christian beliefs. Is this something we have missed in our doctrines and theological teachings? Does ALL mean ALL when God says it?)

Verse 2: *"And he had in his hand a little book open: and he set his right foot upon the sea, and his left foot on the earth,"*

The "right" side of anything in Scripture speaks of the power and authority of God. The "left" side is not excluded from God but functions in a different realm. Remember that in our previous chapters we discussed the three realms of the temple of God: the outer court (dust), the middle court (sand), and the inner court (star)? These were based on the covenant God made with Abraham.

The picture that John gives us is a corporate body of Christ (star company) coming out of the heavenly realm manifesting their god identity in the flesh. They are reflecting the power and authority of God to the middle court (Pentecostal realm), and the carnal man (outer court). What is this power and authority? THE MERCY SEAT OF GOD filled with the Love of God.

The foundation of the "angel" or corporate body is in the sand (sea) and in the dust (earth). God is not eliminating people, but incorporating them because the death and resurrection of Jesus Christ was not for a few willing to receive, but for all humanity. God placed eternity (Himself) within each of us (Eccl. 3:11).

The seventh angel in this chapter has a message "upon" or at a higher realm of understanding than the carnal Christian (earth), and the double-minded Pentecostal (sea) declaring from heaven we have already been blessed with all spiritual blessings in heavenly places (Ephesians 1:3). Today, we are new creatures in Christ and the old Adam does not exist anywhere or in any person because Jesus paid the price of sin and death for ALL humanity whether we acknowledge it or not (2 Corinthians 5:17). The birthright has been given, the blessing is optional.

"For it is written: "As I live, says the Lord, every (ALL) knee shall bow to Me, and every (ALL) tongue shall confess to God." (Romans 14:11)

"At the name of Jesus every (ALL) knee should bow, of those in heaven, and of those on earth, and of those under the earth, and that every (ALL) tongue should confess that Jesus Christ is Lord, to the glory of God the Father" (Philippians 2:10-11).

The word "blessing" that Paul used in Ephesians 1:3 is the Greek word "Eulogia" meaning, "to declare as indwelt by God and thereby **fully** satisfied." It is NOT the Greek word "makarismos" which means "the action of becoming blessed." The blessing Paul is telling us about is the inheritance we have now because of the death of Jesus Christ; not a blessing we will receive someday when we die.

A "eulogy" are words said over someone that is dead. The Holy Spirit is telling us that we were dead in sin, but today we are alive in Christ. People like the idea of "dying daily" because it gives them a back door of excuses to keep missing the mark from being who they really are as a son of God and the responsibility required with this revelation. Unconditional love, mercy, and grace come up against religious justification. This process will force us to rest in heavenly places and live by faith (Hebrews 4:3).

The "little book" is the same book we discussed in Revelation chapter five that was in the right hand of Jesus Christ while he sat on the throne. It is the Holy Bible as He knew called the Tanakh – the Torah, prophets and wisdom writings of the Old Testament, not the King James version or New Testament. It is the Revelation of Jesus Christ; it is Christ in you the hope of glory that when we read the Tanakh we should see the WORD made flesh written on our hearts (Hebrew 8:8-10). John is the same author who wrote in John 21:25, *"And there are also many other things which Jesus did, the which, if they should be written every one, I suppose that even the world itself could not contain the books that should be written."* We are those books, the living epistles of Christ today (2 Corinthians 3:1-3).

In Chapter 5, the book was sealed and only the Lamb of God was worthy to break the seals. Remember, Jesus died for the sins of the whole world. What He accomplished and finished for you and me was also done for all humankind (Hebrews 10:10). We have established that the Book of

John is using a Hebrew method of teaching called "Remez"- going back to move forward. The reference to seals is a description of a Torah scroll that is made out of lamb's skin.

Revelation is the Revelation of Jesus Christ (Rev. 1:1); however, it is not just about the man Jesus who walked on this earth but also about the corporate body of Christ being unveiled as the Lamb breaks the seals so that Christ would be manifested all in ALL (Colossians 3:11). As we go through each chapter, we see each layer of the unveiling of *"Christ in you, the hope of glory"* (Col. 1:27). We are the house of God going through the building process. The seals are only temporary until we reach a certain place of growth in Christ so that each particular seal can be broken off and we can move into each new realm of relationship with God.

Verse 3: *"And cried with a loud voice, as when a lion roareth: and when he had cried, seven thunders uttered their voices."*

This "angel" or corporate body of Christ is declaring a message. It is one message (a loud voice) being heard through many that are manifesting the mind of Christ. The "lion" is symbolic of power in this message. The number seven symbolizes a complete message; and the word "thunders" tells us that this message is released in the earth. The sound of thunder actually happens at the same time that lightening occurs, yet often times we don't see or hear them together because of the distance of the event.

Verse 4: *"And when the seven thunders had uttered their voices, I was about to write: and I heard a voice from heaven saying unto me, Seal up those things which the seven thunders uttered, and write them not."*

Reading this verse may sound confusing because if this is a message for all humanity to be set free then why wouldn't John be allowed to write about it? The message of "Christ in you, the hope of glory" has been released to humanity since the resurrection of Jesus Christ. The wisdom for us to know that mankind was **created as a son of God** has been written since the Book of Genesis. So why have we been subjected to years of double-minded doctrine calling it Christianity?

The perfection of all that God had created was completed before the foundation of the world (Ephesians 1:4). *"Thus the heavens and the earth were finished, and all the host of them* (all of creation). *And on the seventh day God ended his work which he had made; and he rested on the seventh day from all his work which he had made. And God blessed the seventh day* (completed work), *and sanctified it* (made it perfect): *because that in it* **(all creation)** *he had rested from all his work which*

God created and made" (Genesis 2:1-3.) This is what John was about to write in Rev. Chapter 10, but could not because the plan of God for manifesting this perfection fullness must first be experienced in us to go through a process of growth and development so the testimony of Christ can then be written.

The ways of God are not man's ways. How could we understand a father's love for his children who gives them a serpent to play with? We would not have even created it to begin with let alone have it in our backyard. Yet, God placed the Tree of Knowledge of Good and Evil right in the middle of the garden knowing that man would be tempted. We know that God is love and in Him, there is no darkness. He is not a vindictive Father, so we must conclude that this whole picture has a greater blessing than we can comprehend with our natural understanding. Therefore, our rest comes by trusting and walking in faith by the example that Jesus gave us as He reveals that we have the mind of Christ to live and be as He is today (1 John 4:17).

John tells us in the verse that he heard the message, but was not allowed to write what he heard. The name "John" means "gracious." We each must come through an understanding revealed to us as the seals are broken from the hardness of our hearts by the Holy Spirit that the free gift of our salvation is only by the grace and mercy of God that **He gave to us. We did nothing!** Whether we receive this gift or not does not matter to God or change His perfect and completed work. However, we must remember that the laws of nature reveal that everything goes through seasons of growth to come into maturity. This is why a grandmother can be at peace when she sees mischievousness in her grandchildren, yet mom is going through the frustration of how to be a parent to her children. *"Beloved, now we are children of God; and it*

In the seasons of change, we only see partially, but when the next season comes, we can see clearly what we were to experience in that season to equip us for our next journey.

has not yet been revealed what we shall be, but we know that when He is revealed, we shall be like Him, for we shall see Him as He is" (1 John 3:2).

In Mark 9, Jesus was confronted with a young boy who could not speak. The disciples tried to cast out the spirit that was causing the problem, but could not. Jesus told them this required fasting **from the disciples, not the young boy.** They had the bloodline of Abraham, yet because of the iniquities of their forefathers which had been passed down through many generations, the disciples needed to cleanse themselves to function properly as Christ ones.

Remember in Rev. 6:9 where we talked about the souls under the altar? These souls had gone through the process of crucifying their natural understanding and are now living and manifesting the mind of Christ. A "dumb spirit" is symbolic of our understanding. When we try to discuss things about our Heavenly Father with our carnal understanding we bring a strange spirit into our thoughts for justifying ourselves in something that is not God. Understanding comes to us individually line upon line, precept upon precept as we grow and develop in Christ. We do not all need to experience the same processing at the same time.

Illustration: There was a generation of the children of God that was born in Egypt. They had 400 years of Egypt culture and customs mingled with their identity as children of God. These people had to go through "processing" an understanding of the ways of God. They needed a wilderness experience of cleansing their minds and hearts of Egyptian culture and customs. They had the identity, but had lost much of the blessings that were given by Jacob/Israel. In their cleansing, they also needed to work through the fact that Joseph's sons had an Egyptian mother. How does this fit into the purity of the bloodline of Israel?

The church has been birthing in the wilderness for over 2000 years "processing" their understanding and development in Christ. We now have a generation that is being birthed in Zion. Those in Zion do not need to experience Egypt or the wilderness to know who they are in Christ. They do not need to rehash what the old Adam did, but build upon the fact that today they are a new creation in Christ. They do need to come to an understanding that the body of Christ is only one church; not churches. It is one body with many members – body parts – around the world (Ephesians 1:1-3).

The processing of 40 years was necessary for the children coming out of Egypt, but was not necessary for Joshua and the generations after that. When Joshua led the next generation born in the wilderness into the promised land given to Abraham, that generation did NOT need to cross the red sea as their parents did to come out of Egypt or the world system. God had already chosen them to go into the promised land while they were uncircumcised. However, they did need to be circumcised to cross the Jordan. This is equivalent to Pentecost, not Passover. As uncircumcised children they would have died and gone to be with the Lord as their parents did. The promised land was their inheritance promised on the earth. They need their hearts circumcised which is related to receiving the WORD written within them, and not just on tablets of stone – pieces of paper found in the Bible.

The historical times of Luther, Wesley, Calvin, and the many other time markers we have through church history have been necessary for us to learn from, but were not meant for placing an understanding of the ways of God in a box. We mistakenly try to force children to grow the same way we did in Christ when they already have the DNA of the revelation of Jesus Christ. Unfortunately, much of what we teach

The church was established at Pentecost, not Passover. For the first and second century they met on the Sabbath of Friday evening to Saturday evening, and they still honored the Torah teachings.

as Christianity today comes from the history of the church around the Constantine era and canonization of the Bible in 381AD. We do not consider the historical inheritance of the church from 33AD with the first Apostles. We don't need forty years in the wilderness, but we do need the 40 days' journey from Passover to Pentecost.

Think about what we see in the natural with the current generation of high school students. They are not required to learn math skills that a calculator can do. They are required to know how to use the calculator. They do not know how to cook on a wood burning stove, but they do know how to use a microwave. Many have no understanding of writing letters because of voice mail and e-mails being available. For the older generations that have camped out in their old way of life it is frustrating because they do not want to learn new things; but for this generation, it is an accepted way of life, not a luxury. Today, it is common for college students to have a computer and know how to use it. This generation would compare taking a computer course a class in learning how to eat or tie your shoes; however, if we go back just one or two generations we will find many people who do not even know how to turn the machine on.

Many of us want to "smite the rock" a second time by justifying ourselves with our way rather than "speaking the word" and believing by faith (Numbers 20). The children in the wilderness went round and round for forty years trying to process the ways of God, yet a harlot in Jericho processed an understanding in one night. She not only understood God's way, but by her understanding, she saved the lives of her whole family, even though they may not have understood what was happening.

Believers today like to enjoy Jesus in a manager at Christmas, celebrate the cross and resurrection at Passover, then take a break and show up at church again for the Christmas season never really developing a quality relationship of knowing God as Father.

Not everything that has been taught by theologians in the past is the whole truth. Remember, it was Moses who smote the rock a second time instead of obeying God to speak to it. Moses went by experiences to bring forth water (the word) instead of the new way that God was telling him. We do this today to the body of Christ and justify to ourselves that it was good enough for us so it will be good enough for the next generation instead of building upon what each generation births. The next generation should not have to suffer the same processing that the previous generation brought forth.

What saves us from pain is getting a "rainbow" on our head. There is a whole lot of "stuff" that we are putting in others and ourselves that is not God. Over three million children of God considered Joshua and Caleb heretics to cross the Jordon into the Promised Land. It took the next generation to do what had been given to the first because they would not stop trying to reason with the ways of God.

Jesus paid a debt He did not owe. We owed a debt we could not pay. My dying to sin is not redemptive. The death, resurrection, and ascension of Jesus Christ paid all debts in full. Today, I am seated in heavenly places ruling and reigning with Him. How about you?

In Matthew 24:45, Jesus tells those who have been placed in authority how they should rule. The first thing to know is how to be a wise and faithful servant to God through Jesus Christ who is the King of kings and Lord of lords. Rulership should only be portrayed as those operating in the mind of Christ.

The second thing to comprehend is that it is God who enlightens us to our identity as sons of God. We did not work for it. In His timing, He has the Holy Spirit pull back the veil allowing us to enter into this identity. The purpose of the unveiling is to bring unity in His household. We are to feed and nurture others with the wisdom and love of the Father in accordance to the season they are in. We do not put ourselves on a pedestal, or force-feed children into the understanding that God gave us.

When we consider the Ark of the Covenant, we have the ability to receive a rainbow on our head (mind of Christ) as we receive the message of how much God loves us. There is a new beginning (life) from a dead tree; legalism (ten commandments) buried in a coffin with mercy and love upon it; bread (supernatural manna) that

> *The cursed fig tree can now produce fruit. The commandments of God become the love language of eternal life. We become the Life giving manna of the body of Christ.*

feeds us in supernatural ways. Our spirit, soul, and body can receive life, life, and life; a three bonded scarlet cord in our hearts shining out through the windows of our lives to display just how much God loves us. It is not by our power or our might, but by the word of God within that enables us to give love to others. This love will in turn cause transformation in them.

John challenges us to come up to a higher place; to leave behind illusions, falsehoods, and fears pertaining to the ways of God. This is not a new message, but one that had been unveiled from the beginning when Moses wrote the first five books of the Bibles. We read in Deuteronomy 30:11-14, *"Now what I am commanding you today is not too difficult for you or beyond your reach. It is not up in heaven, so that you have to ask, "Who will ascend into heaven to get it and proclaim it to us so we may obey it?" Nor is it beyond the sea, so that you have to ask, "Who will cross the sea to get it and proclaim it to us so we may obey it?"* **No, the word is very near you; it is in your mouth and in your heart so you may obey it"** (NIV).

"But put ye on the Lord Jesus Christ, and make not provision for the flesh, to fulfill the lusts thereof" (Romans 13:14). We must feed on Lamb to be able to follow the example that Jesus gave us on how to be in the world, but not of it.

In 2 Chronicles 7:14 God said, *"If my people, which are called by my name, shall humble themselves, and pray, and seek my face, and turn from their wicked ways;* **then will I hear from heaven**, *and will forgive their sin, and will heal their land."* Most theologians use this verse to justify how bad people in the world exist today. God is not elaborating on how wicked man is, but declaring that there is an identity in us that needs to come out so that we can have full fellowship with Him as His family. God desires to hear the words that we speak from our mouths to be His realm of wisdom and understanding that can only be found in the inner court where the mercy seat is located. If we were to enter this domain with any "self-ego", we would immediately be destroyed. However, in order for God to commune with His own identity, His sons and His wife must hear a heavenly mindset coming from our hearts and mouths with His voice. Anything less we are like children needing to be taken care of, or young adults between puberty and teens being tossed back and forth.

When we talk from heaven, we are declaring to the natural how it already is "in Christ." When we pray, "if it be thy will" we are speaking from an earthly understanding determined by the "woes" around us. Paul says that we **have been** blessed by God *"with all spiritual blessings in heavenly places in Christ"* (Ephesians 1:3). It is not something we receive someday when we die. It is up to us to appropriate these blessings into our lives.

Verse 5: *"And the angel which I saw stand upon the sea and upon the earth lifted up his hand to heaven"*

This is a beautiful picture for us to remember. The corporate sons of God are in a position of worshipping to the Father. By knowing their identity in Christ, they have received from Father God the ability to give unconditional love to those with Pentecostal understanding (sea), and those with carnal (earth) mindsets. They are likened to pipe vessels which direct the love, hope, and encouragement of God to all those who cross their path.

Love, joy, and peace are spiritual realities; not emotional highs. They are the outward manifestation of the mind of Christ; not the result of information accumulated by the senses. In the book of James, we are told, *"My brethren, count it all joy when ye fall into divers temptations; knowing this, that the trying of your faith worketh patience. But let patience have her perfect work, that ye may be perfect and entire, wanting nothing. If any of you lack wisdom, let him ask of God, that giveth to all men liberally, and upbraideth not; and it shall be given him. But let him ask in faith, nothing wavering. For let not that man think that he shall receive any thing of the Lord."* (James 1:2-7). Counting it ALL joy in diverse temptations cannot be obtained with our natural understanding. It takes faith! We have to draw on the resurrection power of Jesus Christ: *"That I may know him and the power of his resurrection"* (Philippians 3:10).

Verse 6: *"And swore by him that liveth for ever and ever, who created heaven, and the things that therein are, and the earth, and the things that therein are, and the sea, and the things which are therein, that there should **be time** no longer:"*

Time was created for man. Eternity is our identity in Christ. Freewill allows us to choose how much eternity we desire to bring into our time.

This corporate company of firstfruits is declaring the message about the mediator between heaven and earth. God created all things and is in all things that He created. *"For there is one God, and one mediator between God and men, the man Christ Jesus; who gave himself a ransom for all, to be testified in due time"* (1 Timothy 2:5-6). God establishes the perfect timing to reveal the greatness of His love and mercy for the purpose of manifesting Christ in us: *"**When it pleased God**, who separated me from my mother's womb, and **called me by his grace**, to reveal his Son in me, that I might preach him among the heathen"* (Galatians 1:15-16).

The revelation of Jesus Christ in me is not about me or about my salvation. It is about the unveiling of Christ in all humankind including me. *"For as in Adam all die, even so in Christ shall all be made alive. But every man in his own order: Christ* (Jesus) *the firstfruits; afterward they that are Christ's* (manifesting their identity as a son of God) *at his coming* (when the Holy Spirit reveals to them, Christ in you). *Then cometh the end* (not the end of the world, but the end of time controlling us), *when he shall have delivered up the kingdom to God* (the realm around us radiates with His identity), *even the Father; when he shall have put down all rule and all*

> *"God is Light"*
> *(I John 1:5.) Light energy has different frequencies that range from long radio wavelengths to pinpoint short waves of Gamma Rays. So it is with the WORD, from literal to spiritual where the thought becomes the fact (Proverbs 23:7).*

authority and power (religion; legalism; justification through the misuse of the Father's words). *For he* (Jesus Christ is the head) *must reign, till he* (the corporate body of Christ) *hath put all enemies* (antichrist spirit) *under his* (Christ) *feet"* (1 Corinthians 15:22-25).

Verse 7: *"But in the days of the voice of the seventh angel, when he shall begin to sound, the mystery of God should be finished, as he hath declared to his servants the prophets."*

The word "days" is not a literal 24-hour period, but a time in each of our lives when we come into the DAY OF THE LORD. It will be a different time for each of us, but we will all come into it. It is a corporate word, but we hear it individually. Paul tells us in 1 Corinthians 15:21-23, *"For since by man came death, by man came also the resurrection of the dead. For as in Adam all die, even so in Christ shall all be made alive. But every man in his own order: Christ the first fruits; afterward they that are Christ's at his coming."*

The mystery of God was no longer hidden behind a veil after Jesus said, "It is finished" on the cross (John 19:30). What did Jesus finish? What was known by all the prophets that was spoken hundreds of years earlier that Jesus would bring a completion of? He removed the bondage that hindered us from knowing *"It is Christ IN YOU, the hope of glory"* (Col. 1:27) which has been place in seed form by God in all humankind and can now be manifested. It is not a message for just the Jewish nation, and it is not a message for someday when we die and go to be with the Lord. We are already in His presence NOW with access to the fullness of our inheritance.

> *John the Baptist prophesied before baptizing Jesus, "And all flesh shall see the salvation of God" (Luke 3:6).*

Jesus sounded this message to the world while he was stretched out on a cross connecting the gap that separated heaven and earth so that all humanity would come into the understanding of their true identity as sons of God. He (our mediator) finished what He was responsible for in bringing salvation to God's family, mankind credited in HIS image and likeness. He gave us the power and authority as a corporate company of people throughout every generation to do the same by declaring this message. God so LOVED HE gave HIMSELF as a sacrifice to pay the penalty for our sin of missing the mark while we were still sinning and missing the mark in ignorance, pride, and arrogance towards God (John 3:16). It is through His Love released in us that draws men out of their darkness to seek the love of their Heavenly Father who know them before they were conceived in their mother's womb.

Verse 8: *"And the voice which I heard from heaven spoke unto me again, and said, Go and take the little book which is open in the hand of the angel which standeth upon the sea and upon the earth."*

The voice that John is hearing from heaven is coming from the Holy Spirit within him, not the sky. The book is the same one that had been sealed in the previous chapters, but is now open: John is not talking about a literal opening the pages of the Bible and reading the Scriptures, but a quickening of our spirits as love and life transforms us into His image as His sons. The corporate firstfruits of each generation have been carrying this message since the Apostles, but the opposition of receiving it has been from those that have camped in Pentecost (sea) and Passover (earth) realms. They need revelation to see that God already ripped apart the veil that separated them from the throne and mercy of their Father. The New Testament covenant cannot be mixed with the legalism of the Old Testament because this would give us a double-minded understanding of the ways of God. In James 1:8 we are told, *"that a double-minded person is unstable in ALL his ways."*

This corporate man – the bride of Christ - has taken the Scriptures and received the understanding that when the crucifixion took place over 2000 years ago it wasn't just Jesus on the cross, but their lives also; and it wasn't just Jesus who rose from the grave, but they did also. They have already experienced the second death and do not need to die again. *"Always bearing about in the body the dying of the Lord Jesus that the life also of Jesus might be made manifest in our body. For we which live are always delivered unto death for Jesus' sake, that the life also of Jesus might be made manifest in our mortal flesh"*
(2 Corinthians 4:10-11).

Hebrews 2:9-10, *"But we see Jesus, who was made a little lower than the angels for the suffering of death, crowned with glory and honor; that he by the grace of God should taste **death for every man**. For it became him, for whom are all things, and by whom are all things, in bringing many sons unto glory, to make the captain of their salvation perfect through sufferings."*

Just as John had to take the book, we must each come to an understanding that the blessings of our inheritance are not for a someday when we die. Our inheritance is available to us today for the ability to raise others up in the unity of being sons of God by the power and authority of His unconditional love that He has given us.

Verse 9: *"And I went unto the angel, and said unto him, Give me the little book. And he said unto me, Take it, and eat it up; and it shall make thy belly bitter, but it shall be in thy mouth sweet as honey."*

When we believe the message declared by the seventh angel, or corporate body of Christ, opposition will come to everything in our natural understanding. The old mind will fight with justification and tradition trying to overrule what the Spirit of God is declaring in us. If that is not enough, we *This little book is not the whole volume of the Father's teachings in the Torah, but particular versus – Scriptures – that speak LIFE to our spirit at particular seasons in our time in the earth as seeds of the Kingdom.*

can also anticipate from those around us to separate them from us as we declare this message because they will see it as a threat to their misinformed teachings about heaven, hell, and "freewill." They will challenge our soul by calling us "heretics" and "new age" using doctrines and theological hierarchy to justify their position. For those that know they are sons of God, they will find themselves many times isolated and baffled as to why others do not want to receive the unconditional love of God.

The reality of "hell" will become open to their soul and they will learn that it is not about going some place with demons and dragons, but living our lives today as Paul taught us in Galatians, *"But if, while we **seek to be justified by Christ** (freewill theology), we ourselves also are found sinners, is therefore Christ the minister of sin? God forbid. For if I build again the things which I destroyed, I make myself a transgressor. For I through the law am dead to the law (religious understanding of Scripture), that I might live unto God. I am crucified with Christ: nevertheless I live; yet not I, but Christ liveth in me: and the life which I* *now live in the flesh I live by the faith of the Son of God, who loved me, and gave himself for me.* **I do not frustrate the grace of God** (with the doctrine of freewill or works): *for if righteousness comes by the law, then Christ is dead in vain"* (Galatians 2:17-21).

Verse 10: *"And I took the little book out of the angel's hand, and ate it up; and it was in my mouth sweet as honey: and as soon as I had eaten it, my belly was bitter."*

As the bitterness of turmoil and confusion challenges our minds; our hearts will speak forth the sweetness of His mercy and love bringing us the peace that surpasses our understanding knowing that His word will not return unto Him void. Our words will become sweet as honey to those that God has prepared to receive their inheritance. Those who do not hunger and thirst for the Father's presence will find the Torah offensive justifying in their heart that they do not need instruction.

> *The law of sin and death was paid for all mankind by the blood of Jesus Christ. The Torah is now an open invitation through the Salvation we obtain through Jesus Christ to hear the Father's love and guidance by His Spirit to train up a child in the way he should go to rule and reign with the Father on the earth.*

Verse 11: *"And he said unto me, Thou must prophesy again before many peoples, and nations, and tongues, and kings."*

Theologians have frequently misused the word "prophesy." It literally means to "speak under the inspiration of the Holy Spirit." Whenever we speak the word of God, with the character and nature of our Heavenly Father, we speak under the inspiration of the Holy Spirit. Jesus was called the prophet, the priest, and the king, but he never went anywhere saying, "Thus saith the Lord" because he knew his identity in God. This is the example we are supposed to follow in BEING the light where the Holy Spirit takes us. Our words become His words so that when others see us, they see their Heavenly Father.

When we speak the word of the Lord in His character and nature, it tears down some things and brings up other things. Controversy should not be a surprise to us because the word of God is sharper than a two-edged sword dividing and piercing the soul and spirit. The only thing that can enter the Holy of Holies is SPIRIT, which means the soul has to be separated so that it will no longer control and be the justifier of our being. The WORD of God can only do this. John is writing the fulfillment of what Ezekiel prophesied:

Ezekiel 2:5-3:4:

> *"And they, whether they will hear, or whether they will forbear, (for they are a rebellious house,) yet shall know that there hath been a prophet among them. And thou, son of man, be not afraid of them, neither be afraid of their words, though briers and thorns be with thee, and thou dost dwell among scorpions: be not afraid of their words, nor be dismayed at their looks, though they be a rebellious house. And thou shalt speak my words unto them, whether they will hear, or whether they will forbear: for they are most rebellious. But thou, son of man, hear what I say unto thee; be not thou rebellious like that rebellious house: open thy mouth, and eat that I give thee. And when I looked, behold, a hand was sent unto me; and, lo, a roll of a book was therein; and he spread it before me; and it was written within and without: and there was written therein lamentations, and mourning, and woe. Moreover he said unto me, Son of man, eat that thou findest; eat this roll, and go speak unto the house of Israel. So I opened my mouth, and he caused me to eat that roll. And he said unto me, Son of man, cause thy belly to eat, and fill thy bowels with this roll that I give thee. Then did I eat it; and it was*

in my mouth as honey for sweetness. And he said unto me, Son of man, go, get thee unto the house of Israel, and speak with my words unto them."

When we try to understand the prophet's message we must allow the Holy Spirit to bring clarity to the prophesy utilizing the language of the times. When Ezekiel writes the words "house of Israel," he is either speaking to ALL twelve tribes/sons of Jacob/Israel, or to the ten northern tribes/kingdom that went into exile around 700 BC. He would NOT be referring to the southern tribes/kingdom of Judah and Benjamin unless they are being includes as the WHOLE House of Israel. Each tribe had its particular name associated with the particular tribe. Jews were only known through the tribe of Judah and/or the southern kingdom which would include Benjamin. When we identify the name Israel with the Jews only we exclude the other ten tribes that were identified by their regions which today is part of what we know as Israel, yet the northern area was given by God to Ephraim, Reuben, Asher, Zebulun, Manasseh, Naphtali, Dan, Issachar, Simeon, and Gad. This wisdom would have been reflected in the prophesies of the Old Testament.

Notes of Reflection

What were your immediate thoughts in this chapter?

_____
_____
_____
_____
_____

What preconceived thoughts did you have before reading this chapter?

_____
_____
_____
_____
_____

What new information did you learn?

_____
_____
_____
_____
_____

Does this information seem confusing or liberating? Why?

_____
_____
_____
_____
_____

CHAPTER 11

The Two Prophets of God

As we begin in Chapter Eleven, we read that the first verse is connected with Chapter Ten, so let us begin by re-reading the last three verses of the previous chapter:

"And I went unto the angel, and said unto him, Give me the little book. And he said unto me, Take it, and eat it up; and it shall make thy belly bitter, but it shall be in thy mouth sweet as honey. And I took the little book out of the angel's hand, and ate it up; and it was in my mouth sweet as honey: and as soon as I had eaten it, my belly was bitter. And he said unto me, Thou must prophesy again before many peoples, and nations, and tongues, and kings" (Revelation 10:9-11).

The word "prophesy" means to speak under the inspiration of God. If we limit our understanding to John receiving revelation knowledge from God then we limit the blessing that is for us today. John is the disciple or the vessel that God used, but he represents you and me today as Christ upon the earth. As we begin with chapter

What John is sharing is a direct connection with Ezekiel's prophesy concerning the whole house of Israel as the bride of Christ, and the Law of Jealousy found in Numbers 5 along with the woman caught in adultery found in John 8.

eleven, we must realize that we are the ones God is inspiring to speak to "many peoples, nations, tongues, and kings."

Verse One: *"And there was given me a reed like unto a rod: and the angel stood, saying, Rise, and measure the temple of God, and the altar, and them that worship therein."*

This "reed" is symbolic of a measuring tool that has been given to us, the church, to discern "truth" which is being presented to God in His temple. We have been given a measuring stick to measure the temple of God, the altar, and those that worship within. This might sound confusing because we are taught in Matthew chapter seven not to judge. However, if we read beyond the first few verses in chapter seven we find we are to judge righteously.

As we are growing up in Christ, going through the stages of development and maturity that Passover and Pentecost takes us through, we are not to be judging others because we still have areas in our own lives that won't allow us to see fully through the eyes of God's understanding. Once we go into the Holy of Holies we no longer have an opinion of right or wrong because we are dead in Christ, and the life we now live is in Him. When we are seated in heavenly places with Christ, we then have the ability to analyze through the eyes of God to judge righteously. This doesn't mean that we are blinded to what is going on in the world, but that we allow the grace, mercy, and love of

Everyone has life cycle seasons, yet not everyone has the same experience in the same life cycle. What happens to each of us after the flesh dies is only speculation. There are those that left their flesh body, and then returned back into it, but only Jesus Christ literally experience total death to the flesh and was resurrected in a glorified body that never dies. This is our hope of glory today as we enter into His presence.

God to go before us. *"It is the prayers of a righteous man that avails much"* (James 5:16).

The word "temple" is "naios" meaning the Holy of Holies. Spiritually, this would be a person's heart. This is where righteous judgment must take place, not from the position where we judge based on what we see on the outside. Only Jesus Christ has the right to judge from a person's heart. For us to function as kings, priests, and ambassadors for God we must do so with the mind of Christ only; not with a mixture of our own opinions. Only God knows the fullness of an individual's heart and all that is entailed in their life, which would cause positive or negative issues to arise.

The altar is the place of sacrifice. We each must come to a place of sacrifice where we give up all the thought processes that we possess and we now move into what He possesses. The Ark of the Covenant was the place that the High Priest took the offering of blood for the atonement of the sins of the people. Jesus did this for us over 2000 years ago. Today, we are the righteousness of God in Christ whether we believe it or not. This is how we must see others; as Jesus Christ sees us, because He gave His life for the remission of sin once and for all (Hebrews 10:10). We are each being sent out to do the Father's business as Jesus did while He walked the

In Greek theology being "born again" means a one-time experience of receiving Jesus as your personal Savior. In Hebrew theology it means you identify yourself as a child of God (Passover), and continue to have "Mikveh baths" of being born again daily as you enter into His presence with the sacrifice of praise.

earth, but we must also be prepared to go through some wilderness experiences to prepare us for our part of bringing the Kingdom of God into the earth. We must first understand the heart of the Father so that we too can say as Jesus did in John 5, "I only do what I hear the Father say."

The Feast of Passover has a born again experience of coming out of slavery and death into being led by the Spirit of the Lord in our unknown wilderness experience. For some it will seem like hell with no food or water. For others it will be the precious moments of freedom. I have been on many wilderness journeys allowing the Spirit of the Lord to lead. When it is the Holy Spirit leading, one finds themselves surrounded in the presence of peace, unity, and love. Often times I go for long periods of time simply not even thinking of when the last time I ate food or drank water. His presence alone becomes my all that I need at that moment in time.

Biblically, there is a fifty-day journey between Passover and Pentecost refer to as "counting the Omer." It was during this time that Jesus had told the disciples before He went to Calvary that He would see them again in the Galilee which is about a 4-day foot journey north of Jerusalem. We find in Acts 2 where the disciples gathered together in the upper room in Jerusalem which is where the Holy Spirit came upon them on the Day of Pentecost which was also the Day of Shavuot or receiving the Torah on Mount Sinai. This was not by chance, but the instructions they received by Jesus during the forty days He was seen as the resurrection LIFE during the counting of the Omer journey from the Galilee through the wilderness as they went back to Jerusalem. This is a season that the majority of believers who know Jesus Christ as their personal Savior never allow themselves to experience. They know they are born again and going to Heaven when they die. They may have received a prayer language of the Holy Spirit. Yet most believers do not have a daily wilderness experience between Passover and Pentecost. Nor do they realize that there is another wilderness experience after Pentecost to when the Lord returns for His bride who was supposed to be preparing herself for His return. Instead, she is as one of the ten virgins asleep as Jesus describes in Matthew 25.

We are told to measure them that worship. It is not literally "therein" but within what is taking place in their heart. God is Spirit and He seeks those to worship Him in Spirit and Truth (John 4:24). This is the Spirit of Christ in you and the Torah, the Father's teachings and instructions. God is not looking for the outward worship of sacrifice and praise that religion has to offer in the Pentecost and Passover realms. He desires to teach us how to judge righteously by seeing the hearts of His people.

Verse 2: *"But the court which is without the temple leave out, and measure it not; for it is given unto the Gentiles: and the holy city shall they tread under foot forty and two months."*

Everything outside the temple is flesh. We are not talking about a physical temple, but the thoughts and ideas that are created with our natural understanding. We are the temple of the living God, and He dwells within us. Everything that is not God, or is outside of our heart (the mind of Christ) doesn't mean anything! It is only temporary. He said for us to *"leave it out, cast it off and measure it not."* How many of us measure our lives today by the judgments of what occurred in our past? This is all part of the challenge we have to let go of past issues and leave them at the altar in the outer court.

The word "measure" means an affixed standard or a lot by rule. We are only to look at the heart. Isn't that what we would want others to see when we do something wrong? Wouldn't we want them to see the bigger picture of our life with love and grace instead of condemnation? To truly understand the heart of a person it must come from the Spirit of the Lord. Anything else is from the four horseman in Revelation Chapter 6 when the seals were opened. Remember, these seals are the closing ties on the Torah which was made of dead lamb's skins that had been stretched and beaten.

People pay huge amounts of money daily to counselors to confess their dark secrets of their past trying to release the torment they have caused. Many of us will spill our guts to be rid of our demons under the pretense of doctor/patient privacy even though the truth has already been established by Jesus Christ. Only God can forgive sin. The penalty and debt of our past has already been paid through the cross of Calvary. When we receive Jesus Christ as our personal savior we receive the inheritance to supernaturally forgive ourselves and others.

Forgiveness is not saying what someone did wrong is now right. Forgiveness is a supernatural release of the Holy Spirit that allows the iniquities and transgressions to not have any dominion or power in the temple of God and longer.

What would Jesus do when confronted with diverse situations? *"Then answered Jesus and said unto them, Verily, verily, I say unto you, The Son can do nothing of himself, but what he seeth the Father do: for what things so ever he doeth, these also doeth the Son likewise"* John 5:19. So what did the Father tell Jesus to do? *"My brethren, count it all joy when ye fall into divers' temptations; knowing this, that the trying of your faith worketh patience. But let patience have her perfect work, that ye may be perfect and entire, wanting nothing. If any of you lack wisdom, let him ask of God, that giveth to all men liberally, and upbraideth not; and it shall be given him. But let him ask in faith, nothing wavering. For he that wavereth is like a wave of the sea driven with the wind and tossed"* (James 1:2-6).

Jesus had to be the manifested WORD of the Father for us to have a visual in order to understand how we are to think and act as sons of God. Jesus had to count it ALL joy so that His words reflected the heart of the Father, for *"A merry heart doeth good like a medicine:"* (Proverbs 17:22), and *"a merry heart hath a continual feast"* (Proverbs 15:15). In everything that Jesus was confronted with he had to find *"the joy of the Lord* (his Christ identity) *as his strength"* (Nehemiah 8:10).

We must know that we now have God's heart, or the mind of Christ, in order to see the creation of God through His eyes. If we try to understand the ways of our Father with our natural mind, also known as an old stony heart, we will speak words from *"our heart that proceeds evil thoughts, murders, adulteries, fornications, thefts, false witness, blasphemies: These are the things which defile a man"* (Matt 15:19-20).

Words are the fruit that comes off of the two trees in the midst of the Garden or the midst of the heart of the matter. Circumcision of the heart is a process of discerning the difference between what is "good" from the Tree of Knowledge of Good and Evil and what is "good" from the Tree of Life.

"For the word (Christ in us) *of God is quick, and powerful, and sharper than any two edged sword, piercing even to the dividing asunder of soul and spirit, and of the joints and marrow, and is a discerner of the thoughts and intents of the heart"* (Hebrews 4:12).

"And the holy city shall they tread underfoot forty and two–months."

Today, we have the ability to walk in the power and authority of the mind of Christ. The "holy city" shall be our lifestyle; the place of His residence in us. Forty-two months are equivalent to three and one-half years. This is not a literal number. This number has a spiritual significance we are supposed to connect with in relationship to the ministry of Jesus while he walked the earth. It also represents the 42 generations that natural Israel (our flesh) was in oppression before Jesus Christ.

The whole time that humanity is on this earth is a time of ministry. The whole time we are in our natural body is a time of ministry. The Spirit of God is ministering to each of us in the Spirit and using the flesh to help us overcome our imagination. We are not to give place to the flesh's way because it doesn't count with God, but we are to

Often times we confuse a ministry calling for the Lord with friendships. Friendships are a network support system that gives and takes in both directions of receiving and giving. A ministry is a giver with no expectation of receiving for their source comes from the Father's heart, not man.

remember that God uses the natural for us to understand His ways (1 Corinthians 15:46). Our focus as an overcomer is to be upon the heart of humanity as Jesus demonstrated rather than the outer appearance.

We are told by Solomon in Ecclesiastes Chapter Three that "time" is a temporary vessel created by God for the purpose of maturing into our true identity in Him. If something can be affected by time, then it is not real, but an illusion. Maturing in Christ comes to the understanding that only the WORD will last forever. *"As He is, so are we in this world"* (1 John 4:17). Jesus Christ is the living Torah, the WORD made flesh and dwells among men (John 1:14). We too are meant to be bone of His bone and flesh of His flesh, the living Word in us manifested in the earth. We were never meant to be a denomination or building of mortar and bricks to house people in, but a community of one body in Christ functioning with our God given gifts and talents to bring unity to the many members of the body so that only Jesus Christ is glorified in the earth.

Verse 3: *"And I will give power unto my two witnesses, and they shall prophesy a thousand two hundred and threescore days, clothed in sackcloth."*

The words "power and unto" are not in the original. The verse should say "I will give of me two witnesses." This means that there will be a witness of God in the earth. The number "two" is not a literal two people but a spiritual number meaning "union and division."

Only the word of God is true prophesy. 2 Peter 1:20-21 tells us, *"Above all, you must understand that no prophecy of Scripture came about by the prophet's own interpretation. For prophecy never had its origin in the will of man, but men spoke from God as they were carried along by the Holy Spirit"* (NIV). It is a sword that divides and unites. *"For the word of God is quick, and powerful, and sharper than any two-edged sword, piercing even to the dividing asunder of soul and spirit, and of the joints and marrow, and is a discerner of the thoughts and intents of the heart"* (Hebrews 4:12).

God will give His word of truth to those clothed in sackcloth or humility and grief. This is not someone that is penniless and depressed, but those that have put aside their own feelings, emotions, and natural understanding to lift up the ways of God that will unite and edify the body of Christ. Again, the number; one-thousand two hundred and three score days (42 months), is symbolic of the lives of each generation being a ministry for God's purpose and plan so that He will be glorified all in ALL.

Verse 4: *"These are the two olive trees, and the two candlesticks standing before the God of the earth."*

We can go to Zech. 4:11-14 to find a witness about these candlesticks and olive trees:

"Then answered I, and said unto him, what are these two olive trees upon the right side of the candlestick and upon the left side thereof? And I answered again, and said unto him, what be these two olive branches which through the two golden pipes empty the golden oil out of themselves? And he answered me and said, Knowest thou not what these be? And I said, No, my lord. Then said he, these are the two anointed ones that stand by the LORD of the whole earth."

Then when we read in Romans 11:15-26:

> *"For if the firstfruit be holy, the lump is also holy: and if the root be holy, so are the branches. And if some of the branches be broken off, and thou, being a wild olive tree, wert grafted in among them, and with them partakest of the root and fatness of the olive tree; Boast not against the branches. But if thou boast, thou bearest not the root, but the root thee. Thou wilt say then, the branches were*

broken off, that I might be grafted in. Well; because of unbelief they were broken off, and thou standest by faith. Be not high minded, but fear: For if God spared not the natural branches, take heed lest he also spare not thee. Behold therefore the goodness and severity of God: on them which fell, severity; but toward thee, goodness, if thou continue in his goodness: otherwise thou also shalt be cut off. And they also, if they abide not still in unbelief, shall be grafted in: for God is able to graft them in again. For if thou wert cut out of the olive tree which is wild by nature, and wert grafted contrary to nature into a good olive tree: how much more shall these, which be the natural branches, be grafted into their own olive tree? For I would not, brethren, that ye should be ignorant of this mystery, lest ye should be wise in your own conceits; that blindness in part is happened to Israel, until the fullness of the Gentiles be come in. And so all Israel shall be saved: as it is written, There shall come out of Zion the Deliverer, and shall turn away ungodliness from Jacob: For this is my covenant unto them, when I shall take away their sins."

The double witness of what God is doing is found in the Old Testament and New Testament. The Old Testament represents our carnal understanding or people that want to play religious games with God and His children. They didn't care about God; they just wanted their rules, regulations, doctrines, and creeds to control the body of Christ. The New Testament is a witness to God using people such as Paul who were grounded in religion to go to those that had no relationship with God. This is not about the nation of Israel on one side and the Church on the other as most pastors preach. This is about two kinds of people. People who love God with a relationship of knowing Him as Father, and people who play games with God in their Christian walk with a mixture of grace and law.

We have previously studied about the candlesticks being representative of the church's characteristics. In this verse, speaking of two candlesticks would mean a witness about the church. This is not literally two buildings somewhere on earth, but the true church or body of Christ versus those that represent Christianity by a doctrine or tradition surrounded by a building. There have always been people who are sincere in the body of Christ and those that are not. This is the double witness that has always been around. It is God's word that separates and divides the real from the false for us to know the true bride of Christ. The body of Christ must be connected with the mind of Christ that Jesus demonstrated when he ministered for 42 months.

What we refer to as the New Testament is actually not new, but the renewed covenant teachings of the Torah taught by Jesus as the Father's love language and not a law.

Verse 5: *"And if any man will hurt them, fire proceedeth out of their mouth, and devoureth their enemies: and if any man will hurt them, he must in this manner be killed."*

The word "man" refers to our carnal mind. "Hurting them" is referring to the double witness of the Old and New Testament. The Bible is a book of LIFE, LOVE, and LIGHT. It should be appropriated as our Heavenly Father's love letters' teaching us how to grow in His grace and mercy uniting all humankind together with no condemnation. When the word of God is used to justify, separate, or condemn ourselves or others God calls it a wickedness that must be removed. If we would only realize that the many issues of frustration that we are burdened with about others may be to change us, not them. Paul was confronted with *"thorns in his flesh"* three times until he surrounded to the will of God that *"His grace was sufficient."* When Scripture is used to justify, separate, or condemn ourselves or others, God calls it a wickedness that must be removed. God is a consuming fire. It is His word in us that will both judge and purify our natural mind manifesting the Christ identity we each already possess.

"He must in this manner be killed." God does not need to literally kill anyone for transformation to take place within us. "This manner" is connecting us to the word that was used for justification against another. This judgment of others will be used to judge our own hearts. Jesus said in Matthew 7:1-2, *"Do not judge, or you too will be judged. For in the same way you judge others, you will be judged, and with the measure you use, it will be measured to you"* (NIV).

Verse 6: *"These have power to shut heaven that it rain not in the days of their prophecy: and have power over waters to turn them to blood, and to smite the earth with all plagues, as often as they will."*

As a new creation in Christ the old man is dead. This death must be viewed as being in a coffin and people are talking negatively about us, yet we do not respond because we are dead.

Theologians like to consider these two witnesses as being Elijah and Moses. The problem with this teaching is it isn't applicable for us today. It causes us to take what John wrote and justify what we think he might have been writing about instead of considering it as a personal connection.

The phrase "The Way" is a Hebrew word "Derek" which means, "Your intimate journey with God."

Having power to shut heaven is referring to the Spirit realm. If we take just the Old Testament or just the New Testament and use it to justify our Christian life we are shutting out the inner court of our existence and staying within the Passover and Pentecost understanding. We are placing boundaries around our lives limiting the Christ identity that is already established within us. The Old Testament has historical understanding, but it also must be viewed as spiritual application for each of us today. There should be a continuous spiritual flow in our hearts from the Old Testament to the New Testament. The layout of the Scriptures that have a piece of paper separating the Old and New should not be the application of how we interpret the Bible. Jesus used the Old Testament to teach from, and Paul was a Rabbi taking the Old Testament teachings and making them relevant as a love language of the Father through Jesus Christ.

The reference to "rain" from the Spirit realm refers to the Word of God. When Scripture is applied to in the first two realms (body and soul) of whom we are our emotions, or the senses of our flesh, are being consulted. We are judging by the outward appearance instead of righteously with the eyes of God. To judge righteously knowing if God is speaking to someone, or whether or not the Holy Spirit is really moving on an individual, we must be sitting in the Holy of Holies on the mercy seat of God with the mind of Christ.

Having power over waters is using the word of God to justify and kill the flesh with our natural understanding. Scriptures are being used to control these two realms instead of allowing Spiritual waters from heaven to draw people out of the wickedness and bondage of their carnal minds. Paul tells us in 2 Corinthians 3:3-6, *"Forasmuch as ye are manifestly declared to be the epistle of Christ* (the WORD) *ministered by us, written not with ink, but with the Spirit of the living God; not in tables of stone, but in fleshy tables of the heart. And such trust have we through Christ to God-ward: Not that we are sufficient of ourselves to think any thing as of ourselves; but our sufficiency is of God; Who also hath made us able ministers of the new testament; not of the letter, but of the spirit: for the letter killeth, but the spirit giveth life."*

The plagues upon the earth are symbolic of the trials and tribulations we will all encounter individually and corporately as the birthing process for us to be transformed into the perfect bride of Christ. This is not speaking of

Plagues bring us to the crossroads of life. Do we deal with them horizontally from our past to future, or do we seek wisdom vertically from Heaven to earth?

natural disasters or the CNN reports that may occur around the world because we think that God is angry at humanity and as a result will destroy us. Instead, the "plagues" will put pressure on each of us to chasten and correct us because He loves us so much knowing that the old carnal mind must be exposed to prevent harm. Let's read a few verses of what Scripture is telling us about tribulation:

Acts 14:22, *"Confirming the souls of the disciples, and exhorting them to continue in the faith, and that we must through much tribulation enter into the kingdom of God."*

Romans 2:8-11, *"But unto them that are contentious, and do not obey the truth, but obey unrighteousness, indignation and wrath, Tribulation and anguish, upon every soul of man that doeth evil, of the Jew first, and also of the Gentile; But glory, honor, and peace, to every man that worketh good, to the Jew first, and also to the Gentile: For there is no respect of persons with God."*

Romans 5:2-5, *"By whom also we have access by faith into this grace wherein we stand, and rejoice in hope of the glory of God. And not only so, but we glory in tribulations also: knowing that tribulation worketh patience; And patience, experience; and experience, hope: And hope maketh not ashamed; because the love of God is shed abroad in our hearts by the Holy Ghost which is given unto us."*

> **The word Gentile in the New Testament is translated as those confused and without a relationship with God. In the Old Testament the word refers to the northern 10 tribes of Israel that were not abiding in God's teachings in the Torah.**

2 Corinthians 1:3-5, *"Blessed be God, even the Father of our Lord Jesus Christ, the Father of mercies, and the God of all comfort; Who comforteth us in all our tribulation, that we may be able to comfort them which are in any trouble, by the comfort wherewith we ourselves are comforted of*

God. For as the sufferings of Christ abound in us, so our consolation also aboundeth by Christ."

God is not trying to punish us, but is bringing us into maturity. This is done through tribulations or pressures in our life causing us to change from the way we would handle situations with our natural understanding.

In the Book of Joel we are given an illustration of different stages of the locust. These stages are symbolic of the different growth periods we will be confronted with as we mature in Christ.

> ➤ **Palmerworm:** means to devour, shearer; strong stand in religious traditions found in the outer-court. These are born-again believers in Jesus Christ that have crossed through Passover, but not willing to take the journey through the wilderness to Mt. Sinai/Mt. Zion for Pentecost.
> ➤ **Locust/grasshopper:** to increase, multiply swarm. This is the Pentecostal/revival groupies. The "spirit-filled," but strong in the carnal understanding.
> ➤ **Cankerworm/caterpillar:** this creature has small wings to leap, but not fly; it devours. This stage is sin conscious while in the Pentecostal mind. They are dualist in their understanding of the ways of God.
> ➤ **Full-grown caterpillar/the ravager:** This stage is a consuming locust or finisher. The belief is in third day/kingdom now, but they still carry traditions. "Sonship" is singular, not corporate.

Our example to move into the maturity of being a son of God is after the priesthood order of Melchizedek, whom Jesus is the head of. John the Baptist was of the priesthood order, but did not follow the tradition. He ate the Locust as his meat (Matthew 3:4). The complete transformation comes with the bride as a butterfly.

The enemy of God does not care if you are born again because you received Jesus Christ as your personal savior. He doesn't care if you NOW have eternal life and will go to heaven when you die. The "devil, Satan, ego, etc." is the biggest cheerleader for personal salvation. The enemy's concern is when a child of God grows up into the understanding of sonship and the power of his inheritance to unite the body of Christ

> *The corporate body of believers that were gathered together in Acts chapter 2 were unveiling the church, the bride, at Pentecost. They had just gone on a 40-days journey through the wilderness with the resurrected Christ Jesus from Jerusalem to the Galilee and back.*

Verse 7: *"And when they shall have finished their testimony, the beast that ascendeth out of the bottomless pit shall make war against them, and shall overcome them, and kill them."*

The word "testimony" is the word "witness" which comes from the Greek word "marturia" meaning "martyr." A martyr is someone that gives their life for something or someone else. What is the objective for being a Christian today? Those of us that know that our life is hid in Christ have a responsibility to produce the fruit of the Holy Spirit so that His fruit (Galatians 5:22) will be food for others to bring unity to the body of Christ. In order for the "fruit" to be obtainable for the Lord to use, it must be gathered, squashed, and pressed (put in a form of simplicity for a baby to understand). We can't force-feed the wisdom of God to anyone, but we can be an expression of His unconditional love, mercy,

> *In Genesis 1, God spoke to the darkness, then the Holy Spirit moved across the face of the darkness. Then the Light, Life, and Love of God was seen. Our imagination must have the Spirit of God move across our bottomless pit of the unknown.*

and grace as to a child. At the same time, we cannot give away what we do not have. A Passover experience of being born again receives the identity DNA of the Holy Spirit, but without the journey of "counting the omer" and spending time with the resurrected Jesus Christ in the wilderness as the disciples did, trials and tribulations will come upon us and we will seek escapism instead of going through the valley of the shadow of death.

The beast that comes out of the bottomless pit is not a devil with a pitchfork and tail, but the imagination of our own understanding between our ears. As soon as revelation of God flows out of us by the power of the Holy Spirit our carnal mind will challenge us in a subtle way to try to get our ego involved. Be prepared for the war to take place when we are alone and drained from giving the life of God in us to another. Many times this is when we break down, go into depression, cry, and feel anxious and alone. It will seem like an eternity, but really it is exactly where God wants us so that only He can minister and refresh us.

There are many believers in Christ Jesus who profess to be filled with the Holy Spirit, however, because they have not spent time knowing the Father's teachings in the Word, they don't know the voice of the Holy Spirit or familiar spirits of the world.

This beast *"shall overcome and kill them"* is the war in our thoughts and mind that drains us, placing us in a position where we are emptied of all that we are. Let me say again, it is through the many trials we are confronted with which cause us to make a decision to give the unconditional love of God expressed by the fruits of His Spirit that brings us into our inheritance as a son of God. Our spirit and soul may seem to be exhausted and drained allowing us to be vulnerable to be challenged by our ego/beast/devil who will attempt to remove anything left of the power and authority we have in God.

Verse 8: *"And their dead bodies shall lie in the street of the great city, which spiritually is called Sodom and Egypt, where also our Lord was crucified."*

This is not literal "dead bodies." The dead bodies are referring to the children of God not having any power or authority of God. They have been emptied from what authority of God they had; and since they are not mature to "count

Sodom refers to being led by our soul, and Egypt refers to being held as slaves or in bondage to the world system of man.

it ALL joy when trials come" they have allowed the Babylonian spirit of Sodom (flesh) and Egypt (carnal understanding) to dominate their hearts. Paul talks about this in 2 Timothy 3:1-5, *"But mark this: There will be terrible times in the last days. People will be lovers of themselves, lovers of money, boastful, proud, abusive, disobedient to their parents, ungrateful, unholy, without love, unforgiving, slanderous, without self-control, brutal, not lovers of the good, treacherous, rash, conceited, lovers of pleasure rather than lovers of God– having a form of godliness but denying its power. Have nothing to do with them"* (NIV).

Verse 9: *"And they of the people and kindred and tongues and nations shall see their dead bodies three days and an half, and shall not suffer their dead bodies to be put in graves."*

What is taking place here is not a bad thing, but a cleansing of our carnal understanding dominating the body of Christ. Many times we think that we are walking in Christ identity by giving others His unconditional love and mercy, but when we are rejected and alone we become confused and have trouble understanding why someone would not want to receive what we have offered. Jesus and each of the disciples experienced this rejection.

Coming out of Egypt is a Passover experience from death to life. It was a 3-day journey for the children of God to leave Egypt as the Passover family to go into the wilderness and worship God. It was

3 days and 3 nights journey for Jesus to fulfill being the First Fruit of many. Jesus told his disciples that he would see them again in the Galilee before He went to Calvary. That should have been the clue for the disciples to get out of Jerusalem, but they forgot and hid themselves. We have two witnesses/disciples whom Jesus first meets after the resurrection on a journey to Emmaus. Emmaus is not in the direction of the Galilee. These disciples are a husband and wife that witnessed the crucifixion, but not the resurrection. They represent the Adam and Eve of mankind that witnessed the death of eating from the Tree of Knowledge of Good and Evil, but needed the journey back "THE WAY" to return for full restoration of ALL that the enemy had stolen.

Every apostle, prophet, evangelist, pastor, and teacher will go through the separation from others when they try to give the wisdom of God to children only to be spit out like bad food. Many times when we are in a "hand ministry" position we think that this gives us special recognition. However, when people that we try to help treat us like the dust of the earth our senses become confused and we try to justify the situation with our carnal mind. No power and authority of God can flow through the leadership of the church when the carnal senses are in control. There must be an unveiling in our heart to die so that we can live in Christ in His Kingdom now in the earth.

It is only when the "hand ministry" becomes the hand of God (faith, hope, joy, peace, and love) that we have resurrection life flowing through us. The hand is a visual understanding to the ways of God. We are told not to judge (Matthew 7), and if we do then that same judgment will be used toward us. The thumb is likened to the word of God pulling the trigger back. The pointer finger sends the word out, but the middle finger pulls the trigger. It's a balance system. The ring finger is the covenant understanding of the word that was not only sent out to the receiver, but also coming back to the giver with the weapon. The little finger is the foundation. If you try to hold a gun without the last finger it would be very difficult to hit the target.

This finger is the hidden wisdom that all the other fingers depend on: Is the word being sent out with conditions or unconditionally? Is the word of God being sent out for His glory alone as Jesus showed us, or do we have some self-serving issues we are trying to address?

All of this process of cleansing is "spiritual grave time" likened to being buried alive. However, the religious system doesn't want to get rid of those "dead forms" of leadership because it allows the flesh to be in control for a season. In this system, the life of God is not manifested, but Scripture is being used to justify works of the flesh. Many would rather gain an identity in their soul, than let the Spirit of Christ be manifested.

Jesus Christ fulfilled the law of sin and death, and all the prophecies spoken by the prophets. He showed us in the form of a man how to give life that can only come from God. This is something religion can never do. All of creation groans for the manifestation of the sons of God as the Light, Love, and Life of Christ in the earth. The only way we can speak life to one another is when we know who we are in Christ Jesus so that our thoughts are His thoughts and our ways are His ways flowing through us. John tells us in 1 John 4:17 that we must know in our hearts that *as He is, so are we in this world.* If we are going to be able to do greater works than what Jesus did, we will have to step out of the religious system and infuse our life with the Spirit of God.

Verse 10: *"And they that dwell upon the earth shall rejoice over them, and make merry, and shall send gifts one to another; because these two prophets tormented them that dwelt on the earth."*

The "earth" or those that live in the "dust and sand" will rejoice over the tormenting they had received from the prophets or the hand ministry of God. This has been interpreted to mean that the antichrist spirit is going to be glad to see the leadership of the church dead, and then a supernatural occurrence will take place bringing them back to life. If we read this verse again we see that those in the outer and middle court are making merry and sending gifts to one another because they were tormented by the wisdom of God coming from the leadership, not because the leadership is dead. The rejoicing comes because of the signs and wonders being manifested. People in the middle and outer court will seek after these to justify God's word. However, Jesus calls them a "wicked and morally unfaithful generation" (Matt. 16:4). The position of being in the Holy of Holies communing with the Father upon the mercy seat demands death to self and a life of faith NOW that we are one body in Christ. With this understanding, signs and miracles will follow.

Jacob slept on the rock. Moses spoke to it and struck it. Daniel prophesied about the white stone. The Maccabee's hid the stone. Peter is told by Jesus he is the rock.

The word **"tormented"** in this verse means **"touchstone."** A touchstone is a stone used to make a mark on gold or silver to find out what the quality is. The prophets are touchstones that have made a mark on the quality of our salvation (silver), and how much we express the character and nature of our Heavenly Father (gold). If the quality is not pure enough, then we are sent back into the fire to rid the carnal mind so that the life of Christ in us will be manifested.

Verse 11: *"And after three days and an half the Spirit of life from God entered into them, and they stood upon their feet; and great fear fell upon them which saw them"*

The time factor in this verse is not a literal three and a half days, but symbolic of the power of resurrection life that will come forth. It may be one day or it may be several years, but since God's word will not return void, resurrection power will be manifested. God will not share His temple! Signs and wonders are for children, but there will be a time of maturing that no sign is given allowing faith in the word of God to rule and reign.

"They stood upon their feet" is the life and power of God overriding all of our natural understanding. Paul explains this in 1 Corinthians 15:52-54, *"In a moment, in the twinkling of an eye, at the last trump: for the trumpet shall sound, and the dead shall be raised incorruptible, and we shall be changed. For this corruptible must put on incorruption, and this mortal must put on immortality. So when this corruptible shall have put on incorruption, and this mortal shall have put on immortality, then shall be brought to pass the saying that is written, Death is swallowed up in victory."*

"And great fear fell upon them which saw them." Why would there be fear? Whenever we come across things that we don't understand that turns our comfort zone upside down, we put up a defense of fear against the unknown. Religion has taught that we are "sinners saved by grace," and that we have a "free will" to decide if we want to spend eternity in heaven or hell. The Spirit of God comes along and tells us that He is not mad at us, and He wants to set us free from this bondage of works. He tells us that we already have the fullness of our inheritance as a child of His and that there is nothing we can do that will separate us from His love.

> *"Who shall separate us from the love of Christ? Shall tribulation, or distress, or persecution, or famine, or nakedness, or peril, or sword? As it is written, for thy sake we are killed all the day long; we are accounted as sheep for the slaughter. Nay, in all these things we are more than conquerors through him that loved us. For I am persuaded, that neither death, nor life, nor angels, nor principalities, nor powers, nor things present, nor things to come, nor height, nor depth, nor any other creature, shall be able to separate us from the love of God, which is in Christ Jesus our Lord"* (Romans 8:35-39).

When God makes that "touchstone mark" with His word spoken in our hearts, we will go through a time of wrestling with our carnal understanding until we have a peace that surpasses all of our natural thoughts. Only then, will this peace bring forth the resurrection life of Christ in us allowing us to rejoice with a hearts desire to in give the gift of His life to others.

Religion teaches that you can spend your after life in an eternal hell. If God is omnipresent, darkness can't have a place. God is not separated from us, but we allow ourselves to controlled by a lie making the unknown of our imagination greater than God.

Verse 12: *"And they heard a great voice from heaven saying unto them, Come up hither. And they ascended up to heaven in a cloud; and their enemies beheld them."* The "they" is referring to the people that have been wrestling with their carnal understanding of the ways of God. When His peace is received they will hear the voice of the Spirit of God telling them to "COME UP HITHER." This is not dying in a grave to go off somewhere in the sky to a place called heaven. This voice is coming from within us telling us to come to a higher understanding so that the voice of humanity will have no affect. The "enemies" are not people themselves, but their understanding of the ways of God. People who insist upon Christianity being an outer court (knowing God as Almighty) or middle court (knowing God as Father) experience will be in awe with those that come boldly to the throne and sit with Him in the inner court (knowing God as Dad).

"Every knee will bow, and every tongue will confess that Jesus Christ is Lord. All flesh shall see the salvation of God"
Philippians 2:10, Luke 3:6

Verse 13: *"And the same hour was there a great earthquake, and the tenth part of the city fell and in the earthquake were slain of men seven thousand: and the remnant were affrighted, and gave glory to the God of heaven."*

When we first read this verse it is easy to feel uncomfortable about what it means. Many theologians have used it to justify portions of a great tribulation coming. However, let us stay focused on applying this verse to today and what it means personally.

"In the same hour" means at the same time that we are coming into revelation knowledge and relationship with God as our Dad, a "great earthquake" or what is going on in our natural understanding between our ears is going to be shook up and confused. Immediately, our carnal mind will try to take charge and make sense to what God is revealing, but it won't happen because the ways of God seem foolish to our natural thoughts. We will try to "do something" when God is telling us to sit and learn.

> *The longest journey for the Lord, counting the omer from Passover to Pentecost. (Leviticus 23:15-16). This is symbolic of forgiveness mentioned in Matthew 18 in a discussion between Peter and Jesus.*

"The tenth part of the city fell." The tenth is referring to the tithe or the first fruit. God will address the "firstfruit people" or those that He has ordained before the foundation of the world taking them out of the confusion and double-mindedness of religion (city). This is not necessarily those that the church knows as their pastors and teachers, but people that know that *"as He is, so are they in this world."* This is not something that can be taught by man, but revealed by the Holy Spirit for the purpose of uniting the body of Christ. Remember, there

> *When we are searching for God is when we receive revelation knowledge. When we are aware of His presence with us we rest, Selah!*

is only one body of Christ. Jesus died for all humankind fulfilling the sacrificial requirement necessary to unite all people together as one body in Him.

The firstfruits company are the first in their family that believe that Jesus Christ is the Son of God and their Savior. They are not satisfied knowing they are born again and will be going to heaven in their afterlife, but hunger to take the journey of the Lord's feast days established in time to bring eternity of heaven into the earth.

> *"Of his own will begat he us with the word of truth, that we should be a kind of firstfruits of his creatures."*
> *James 1:18*

The "slaying of seven thousand men" is symbolic. Seven is the number of completion or spiritual perfection. It is the number used for the finished work of Jesus Christ. It is the number used for the completion of God's creation. If we were to study this number we would find that all of creation evolves around cycles of seven. A study of the 77 generations of Jesus in the Book of Luke shows a system in which every seventh generation a special man arose. The "thousand" is symbolic of divine completeness and the glory of God. It reveals His divine care and protection for it is His will to bring to perfection that which concerns us allowing us to rest in the wisdom and love that His mercy endures forever (Psalms 138:8).

"The slaying of men" is not a literal killing of people. This is symbolic of the carnal mind, which has lost the battle between the ears, and it is the mind of Christ ruling and reigning in the over-comer. They are able to give glory to God because they know that they are sons of God equipped to do the Father's business while in their natural body.

Again, none of this is a bad thing, but the cleansing of an "antichrist" spirit that has been dominating our mind and heart. Remember, even though we can go through the motions (devotions, tithing, attendance, prayer) of what the church calls being a Christian, there is no power or life in religion. It takes dying to self to be able to come boldly into the throne of God and sit with Him in heavenly places ruling and reigning. The Holy Spirit draws us to "come up higher" to equip us with unconditional love that unites the body of Christ as one; not to make us "holier than anyone else."

Norman P. Grubb states, *"Just keep on the single path. There is nothing but God-in-love, whether appearances are evil or good. HE ONLY is in all of them. Here is the secret."*

Verse 14: *"The second woe is past; and, behold, the third woe cometh quickly."*

Remember, the word "woe" means to stop and really consider what the Lord is doing. Something is going to be done away with, and something is going to change so quickly that if we don't just STOP, we will be confused trying to figure out what happened. There were three woe's spoken of in Chapter 8. We have covered two of these, and very quickly, like a bomb, will be confronted with the third. This is what happens when we enter the outer court, the middle court, and now the inner court of the presence of Father.

When the presence of Christ is fully unveiled there is no past or future revelation. There is only NOW, or being in the moment of eternity in the midst of time.

We must be prepared in our heart as we go through a rapture (outer court experience/identity change); transformation (middle court/life style change); and transfiguration (inner court/resurrection life as an overcomer), to be confronted from the enemy between our ears just as

Jesus was challenged in the wilderness. These occurrences will happen when we are least prepared and equipped with the armor of God.

God is doing a "quick" work in the earth today. What we see around us has its roots in what God is doing within every individual. Whether they acknowledge Him or not, He is requiring His children to grow up in their true identity as His sons. The "wars and rumor of wars" (Mark13:7) are outbreaks of conflict and confusion humanity is confronted with in their heads as they battle with their natural understanding against the wisdom and ways of God. Literally wars have been in existence since time began. John is not writing about the CNN world news as an end time prophesy, but the war we have within ourselves between our ego and Christ in us.

> *The Scriptures unveil to us that God is omnipresence – everywhere all the time, omniscience – all knowing all the time, and Omnipotence – all powerful in Oneness. Where is there a place that God is not? Our imagination.*

Remember the wrestling that Jacob did before his name was changed in Genesis 32: God has given us a new name, but we will each wrestle with ourselves until the power of God in us transforms us into our true identity in Christ.

Verse 15: *"And the seventh angel sounded; and there were great voices in heaven, saying, the kingdoms of this world are become the kingdoms of our Lord, and of his Christ; and he shall reign for ever and ever."*

Again, the number seven is complete or finished. The "great voices in heaven" are one voice called "Christ" that is filling the air with the same message. The battle has been won. I repeat we are not "sinners saved by grace" but "children of the Most High God." The kingdoms are one kingdom identified to BE "righteousness, peace, and joy in the Holy Ghost" manifested from a many-member body called Christ.

Jesus Christ is the head of a many-member body. He is King of kings and Lord of lords. Each cell of His body has the fullness of His DNA and the wholeness of purity found in His bloodline. As a member we cannot stand alone, but must come into the unity of the faith with the mind of Christ Jesus ruling and reigning with Him. "Forever and ever" means into the age of ages. The seed of Christ carried by "firstfruits" will never die even though the vessels of flesh they were carried in may have been limited in time.

I find it amazing that we can now find Holy Ghost wisdom on the internet that was instilled in people during times that they didn't have any understanding of what they had been given. No wonder people were treated like they were crazy and heretics. Can you imagine trying to explain to someone the concept of a microwave who had only been cooking over an open fireplace? Or how about telling someone about cars and planes who only knew the existence of a horse and cart? This is what happens when God gives us something that is so powerful and wonderful that we want to share it with the whole world, but if they are not ready for it they will be offended with you, even though their real battle is with God. You are the messenger or angel being sent by God. The spirit of offense is usually the first weapon the enemy of God will use against the revelation of God's word. Offense will try to shut down the messenger.

Verse 16: *"And the four and twenty elders, which sat before God on their seats, fell upon their faces, and worshipped God,"*

The word "before" in this verse literally means in the mind of God. When we have the mind of Christ, we have the mind of God. The twenty-four elders are symbolic of the complete God man; the government of God; the Rulership of God; the firstfruits.

Notice that the mind of Christ sits on "their" seats? This is taking place in our individual being, not someday after we die. This is today! The word "sitting" identifies a position of resting with Jesus Christ in the midst of the circumstances.

They fell upon their faces is a symbolic illustration of being before God seated in heavenly places. Our identity is in Him. This is also an illustration of giving to God the fullness of His identity, not allowing any "self-ego" to arise. What we put before our face is who we become. After Jacob wrestled with God, he named the place "Peniel" meaning the face of God, or "I have seen God face to face." It is at this point that his name Jacob was changed from "sup planter, schemer, trickster, and swindler" to Israel which means "contender with God."

Verse 17: *"Saying, We give thee thanks, O Lord God Almighty, which art, and was, and art to come; because thou hast taken to thee thy great power, and hast reigned."*

When a couple get married, the woman's name is legally changed at the covenant altar ceremony where she professes her love and commitment to her beloved. The full transformation of her spirit, soul, and body takes place in the inner chamber when she partakes in the consummation of the marriage coming together as one body. When she leaves the bridal/inner chamber she is no longer the bride of Christ, but the wife carrying the seed AND her beloved's name within her body. Selah!

God has taken the power and authority that is in each of us, brought it all together, and He reigns in one body called Christ with Jesus Christ as the head. Let us remind ourselves of what the Scriptures tell us:

"And there are diversities of operations, but it is the same God which worketh all in all" (1 Corinthians 12:6).

"And when all things shall be subdued unto him, then shall the Son also himself be subject unto him that put all things under him that God may be all in all" (1 Corinthians 15:28).

"Which is his body, the fullness of him that filleth all in all" (Ephesians 1:23).

Verse 18: *"And the nations were angry, and thy wrath is come, and the time of the dead, that they should be judged, and that thou shouldest give reward unto thy servants the prophets, and to the saints, and them that fear thy name, small and great; and shouldest destroy them which destroy the earth."*

The "nations" are not literal countries, but the imagiNATIONs that are between our ears. When God comes into our life and takes control, the first thing our carnal mind will do is manifest rebellion against what He is doing because we don't want to give up our control. God said in Deuteronomy 32:21, *"They have moved me to jealousy with that which is not God; they have provoked me to anger with their vanities: and I will move them to jealousy with those which are not a people; I will provoke them to anger with a foolish nation."*

In the Old Testament, the Hebrew nation was considered as a type and shadow for the church system, or body of Christ today. God is provoking us to jealousy **using other people to cleanse us.** How often does our mind battle with thoughts of "If only they would do this, or be this way?" We use so much negative energy with thoughts of

> *The Hebrew nation is made up of all 12 tribes of Jacob/Israel. Not just the tribe of Judah referred to as the Jews.*

accusations trying to change other them when **the purpose of them in your life is to change you!** We read in Numbers 5 the protocol of how to deal with jealousy. This pertains to the suspicion of a husband against his wife possibly having an affair. The wife is challenged by a ritual of words placed on a parchment by the priest which are then placed in water that she drinks. God is a husband to Israel. It is His Word in the Torah that is given to His bride/believers in Christ to take within ourselves. They are sweet as honey, but bitter in our belly. We like to say "thus says the Lord" to others, but when those same words become our judge we find out how much we are the adulteress bride of Christ. This is what we discussed with Revelation 10:10.

The Grace of God is not just sweeping the problem under the rug, but the dunamis power of Christ activated in us that overrides our hurt, confusion, and justification bringing peace that surpasses our natural understanding.

Paul tells us that these are "thorns in the flesh." God doesn't remove these people from our life, but allows them to be a part of the process to change us into understanding that His grace is sufficient in all areas. Be prepared for the imagination to be stirred arousing our emotions to frustration and anger. Remember, this is a cleansing for us to encourage ourselves to grow up in Christ.

"And thy wrath is come." The word "wrath" is not anger the way we understand with our natural mind, but desire and passion that comes from the heart. God is Spirit. There are no sensory emotions connected to God as we know in our flesh. To help us understand the intensity of what is taking place, we are given words like "wrath" to bring forth the depth of God's passion and desire for humanity to bring unity to His body. The natural realm is only a shadow of the depth of how much God loves us. Nothing can separate us from Him:

> *"Who shall separate us from the love of Christ? Shall tribulation, or distress, or persecution, or famine, or nakedness, or peril, or sword? As it is written, for thy sake we are killed all the day long; we are accounted as sheep for the slaughter. Nay, in all these things we are more than conquerors through him that loved us. For I am persuaded,*

> *that neither death, nor life, nor angels, nor principalities, nor powers, nor things present, nor things to come, Nor height, nor depth, nor any other creature, shall be able to separate us from the love of God, which is in Christ Jesus our Lord"* (Romans 8:35-39).

"And the time of the dead." The word "dead" has previously been discussed. Remember, God is Spirit and His word is who He is. Therefore, this word is used to describe those separated from their true identity in Him because of ignorance. Many people; including those that refer to themselves as Christians, are alive in their natural body, but dead to a relationship with God. We each have a time and season we must go through as part of the maturation process. King Solomon tells us in Ecclesiastes 3:1, *"To every thing there is a season, and a time to every purpose under the heaven:"* but when we get down to verse 11 we read, *"He hath made every thing beautiful in His time: also He hath set the world* (eternity) *in their heart, so that no man can find out the work that God maketh from the beginning to the end."*

> **I challenge you to stop and meditate on this. God set HIMSELF (eternity) in our heart. He made everything (ALL) beautiful in HIS time.**

The judgment of the dead is what Jesus did over 2000 years ago at Calvary. He became sin and gave us His righteousness while we were still in ignorance and darkness of understanding or accepting. Judging "sin" is not the issue, but the authority we follow does matter; is it our carnal understanding or the mind of Christ? Our troubles begin with what is in our heart. Jesus corrected the religious authority by saying in Matthew 12:34-37, *"O generation of vipers, how can ye, being evil, speak good things? For out of the abundance of the heart the mouth speaketh. A good man out of the good treasure of the heart bringeth forth good things: and an evil man out of the evil treasure bringeth forth evil things. But I say unto you, that every idle word that men shall speak, they shall give account thereof in the Day of Judgment. For by thy words thou shalt be justified, and by thy words thou shalt be condemned."*

> *As we share the love of God with the Word of God, the Holy Spirit will first convict our hearts asking us, "Are we blessing or judging? Are we truly responding in love or offense?"*

It isn't a matter of what someone does to me, but whether or not I allow them to steal my joy. James tells us in 1:2, *"My brethren, count it all joy when ye fall into divers temptations."* It is our own words that will judge us, not what someone else says or does; is how we respond in our heart.

Verse 19: *"And the temple of God was opened in heaven, and there was seen in his temple the ark of his testament: and there were lightnings, and voices, and thunderings, and an earthquake, and great hail."*

The temple of God is us, not somewhere in the sky. *"What? Know ye not that your body is the temple of the Holy Ghost which is in you, which ye have of God, and ye are not your own? For ye are bought with a price: therefore glorify God in your body, and in your spirit, which are God's"* (1 Corinthians 6:19-20).

"And there was seen in His temple the ark of His testament." The ark represents the presence of God; the Holy of Holies. Only God identity can be in this place. There is no judgment or condemnation in the Holy of Holies, but the fruit of the Holy Spirit that fills every corner: *"love, joy, peace, longsuffering, gentleness, goodness, faith, meekness, temperance"* (Galatians 5:22-23). These attributes are not manifested in us by something that we forcibly try to make happen. His identity (the WORD in our heart) will not share His temple with other words. The attributes of the Holy Spirit will cleanse our hearts as we seek Him, and will fill us with His glory (identity, character, and nature) to give to others. This place today would be the bridal chamber.

The fruit of the Holy Spirit has a growth/development pattern as a baby in the womb. It begins with a foundation of LOVE, layered with JOY. With Joy we received the PEACE of God that surpasses our understanding. We are pregnant, but in the natural we don't see any difference. With love, joy, peace the unveiling of longsuffering comes. The woman's body is going through pregnancy changes that just make her feel nauseated for a season. By the fifth month of pregnancy she has become accepting of the change in her body and her identity with a new titled called "mom." For the next few months the woman will go through the journey of GENTLENESS, GOODNESS, FAITH, MEEKNESS, and finally TEMPERANCE.

"As HE (Christ Jesus) is, so are we today in this world" 1 John 4:17.

Temperance is Christ birthed out of you. When the WORD of God that has been carried in our inner most being/ the womb of mankind, taken time to develop where the mind of Christ in us is in unity with the throne of God/our heart, we give birth to creation LIFE. The WORD comes forth, is circumcised by our heart, and out of our heart the mouth speaks, "LET there BE LIGHT, LIFE, LOVE in the earth." (Galatians 5).

On the Day of Atonement when God was to judge the people of Israel, the representative of the people, the High Priest, went through an intense cleansing ritual for himself before he took on the office of representing the people before God. Jesus has already judged and cleansed all humankind. Who are we to override what He has declared as forgiven and righteous? Today, God does not consider anyone a "sinner" separated from His love. It is the imagination of our own thoughts and ideas that keep us separated from how God really sees us. We are the righteousness of God, not by anything we did or can do, but what He did on Calvary for ALL (2 Corinthians).

"And there were lightnings, and voices, and thunderings, and an earthquake, and great hail." All of these words speak of the revelation of God being manifested in His people. God is light shining

Abortions of babies in the world first began by those that are believers in Christ aborting the LIFE of the WORD of Christ in them with judgment and condemnation in their heart and mind.

through a many-member body called Christ. We are His vessels being used for His word to be spoken. When we speak His truth in the Spirit and identity of the Father, the word released from our mouth will split open the atmosphere around us causing our flesh, or natural understanding, to be shaken. Hail is symbolic of frozen water, or the word of God, hitting the earth (our carnal mind) like mini bombs out of a realm that we can't touch in the natural.

Religion tries to teach us that we have this "freewill" that is more powerful than God's will. If we would stop and think about the love of God in the context of the unconditional love of a father and mother, we begin to see the foolishness of considering that our Heavenly Father, who loves us so much and died for us, would separate us from Himself because we were ignorant to fully understanding His ways. Even in the natural, the law will punish parents for not taking responsibility for their children neglecting them to take care of themselves. If religion were correct with the idea of freewill, then we would be accusing God of neglecting His children.

I end this chapter with Proverbs Three and encourage it to be read as a love letter from our Heavenly Father to teach you in His ways:

> *"My son, do not forget my teaching, but keep my commands in your heart,* (Love the Lord God with all of your heart, soul, and mind) *for they will prolong your life many years and bring you prosperity. Let love and faithfulness never leave you; bind them around your*

neck, write them on the tablet of your heart. Then you will win favor and a good name in the sight of God and man. Trust in the LORD with all your heart and lean not on your own understanding; in all your ways acknowledge him, and he will make your paths straight. Do not be wise in your own eyes; fear the LORD and shun evil. This will bring health to your body and nourishment to your bones. Honor the LORD with your wealth, with the firstfruits of all your crops; then your barns will be filled to overflowing, and your vats will brim over with new wine. My son, do not despise the LORD's discipline and do not resent his rebuke, because the LORD disciplines those he loves, as a father the son he delights in. Blessed is the man who finds wisdom, the man who gains understanding, for she is more profitable than silver and yields better returns than gold. She is more precious than rubies; nothing you desire can compare with her. Long life is in her right hand; in her left hand are riches and honor. Her ways are pleasant ways, and all her paths are peace. She is a tree of life to those who embrace her; those who lay hold of her will be blessed. By wisdom the LORD laid the earth's foundations, by understanding he set the heavens in place; by his knowledge the deeps were divided, and the clouds let drop the dew.

My son, preserve sound judgment and discernment, do not let them out of your sight; they will be life for you, an ornament to grace your neck. Then you will go on your way in safety, and your foot will not stumble; when you lie down, you will not be afraid; when you lie down, your sleep will be sweet. Have no fear of sudden disaster or of the ruin that overtakes the wicked, for the LORD will be your confidence and will keep your foot from being snared. Do not withhold good from those who deserve it, when it is in your power to act. Do not say to your neighbor, "Come back later; I'll give it tomorrow"--when you now have it with you. Do not plot harm against your neighbor, who lives trustfully near you. Do not accuse a man for no reason--when he has done you no harm. Do not envy a violent man or choose any of his ways, for the LORD detests a perverse man but takes the upright into his confidence. The Lord's curse is on the house of the wicked, but he blesses the home of the righteous. He mocks proud mockers but gives grace to the humble. The wise inherit honor, but fools he holds up to shame" (NIV).

Notes of Reflection

What were your immediate thoughts in this chapter?

_____

_____

_____

_____

_____

What preconceived thoughts did you have before reading this chapter?

_____

_____

_____

_____

_____

What new information did you learn?

_____

_____

_____

_____

_____

Does this information seem confusing or liberating? Why?

_____

_____

_____

_____

_____

CHAPTER 12

The Woman Gives Birth to a Son

"And there appeared a great wonder in heaven; a woman clothed with the sun, and the moon under her feet, and upon her head a crown of twelve stars."

Since Chapter 12 begins with the word 'and,' it is necessary to connect chapter 11:19 with this verse: *"And the temple of God was opened in heaven, and there was seen in his temple the ark of his testament: and there were lightnings, and voices, and thunderings, and an earthquake, and great hail…and there appeared…"*

Try to picture the Island of Patmos where John received this revelation from the Holy Spirit: Back then, this island had no artificial lights nearby. After the sun went down and the night darkness surrounded him, John's eyes would have naturally searched for some kind of light. This would have prompted him to look up at the sky to see the formation of the stars. Studying the stars and stargazing was basic knowledge and part of life for most people during this time. Their lives were dependent upon what they saw in the sky. For casual gazers, stars would provide directions and knowledge of seasons. Those that studied the stars would see the story of life being played out in the heavens. It would not have been unusual for John to seek the stars for revelation from God.

John was abandoned on the Island of Patmos because the enemy of God couldn't kill him. However, he would not have been given any scrolls, Tanakh, or Bible for his reading pleasure to receive revelation from the Father. John received what to write by the Holy Spirit speaking to his spirit while the elements of creation in heaven and earth witnessed to what the Father had said in the ancient scrolls taught by Moses and the prophets, and made alive in Jesus Christ.

Today, many of us live so close to areas where there is artificial lighting at night that the splendor of seeing the beauty of the night sky is blinded. However, when we consider John's position, we can see how natural it would have been for him to use star terminology in his writings. It is in this chapter we find the great red dragon that is also talked about in Job 26:13 and Isaiah 27:1. In Job 9:9 we find reference to Arcturus, Orion, Pleiades and the constellations that tell the story of man and the coming Messiah. The Mazzaloth (Zodiac) is found In Job 38:32 where God challenges Job with the message of the stars. Most people will view the stars as a nice wonder of God's creation, but before God's word had been written, the stars were a way God communicated with man.

The phrases: Kingdom of God, Kingdom of Heaven, Son of God, and Son of Man all referred to Jesus Christ. The different phrases were written according to the audience being addressed in the Scriptures.

The writing I am called to do at this time does not allow me to get into a discussion of astronomy, but I suggest that many of us would learn some "great wonders" of the ways of God by reading children's books about the stars and constellations instead of relying on theologians to give us their "end-time" interpretations. Remember, the stars are a natural manifestation of spiritual understanding. God is Spirit, and it is in the spirit realm that we come to understand His way, His truth, and His life.

Verse One: *"There appeared a great wonder in heaven."* Remember, this occurred after the temple of God was opened in heaven. Where is heaven? It is within us, not off in the sky somewhere. A supernatural occurrence is taking place in our spirits. Our natural/logical understanding is a type and shadow of what is going on in the spiritual realm. It is not the end to the means of our understanding, but a small picture of greater things. We read in Matt. 4:16-17, *"The people which sat in darkness* (ignorance) *saw great light* (understanding of God's way)*; and to them which sat in the region and shadow of death* (limitations of time) *light* (eternal) *is sprung up. From that time* (moment; twinkling of an eye) *Jesus began to preach, and to say, Repent* (turn from your natural understanding of the ways of God)*: for the kingdom of heaven is at hand* (now)."

Since heaven has been opened up in us, something occurs with the way we understand Scripture that God calls a "great wonder." Remember, no one can come to Jesus unless the Father draws him (John 6:44). Since we are in Christ, we now possess the mind of Christ to understand and comprehend the ways of our Heavenly Father. However, it takes a severing of our carnal/logical method of reasoning to understand the ways of God. We must also come to the realization that our death is not a coming event, but one that occurred with Jesus at Calvary (Gal. 2:20). The life we should now be living while in the flesh should be His life with His heart's desire and passion to unite the body of Christ in His love, not allowing the idea that Christianity is about self. It should be the Holy Spirit in us that has a voice in our life, and not the familiar spirit of the old self.

"a woman clothed with the sun, and the moon under her feet, and upon her head a crown of twelve stars." The woman can signify an individual, but for the purpose of unity, we must seek a higher understanding. Many have believed that this woman represents natural Israel, but if we study history, Israel was never in the heavens. This woman represents the church; the body of Christ; the bride of Christ; the "freewoman" of Paul's allegory (Gal. 4:21-31).Who is she clothed

with? She is clothed with the sun who is symbolic of the CHRIST; the son of righteousness, the Light of the world (Mal. 4:2; John 8:12).

The moon represents a few things here: The law of sin and death, the powers of darkness, and or the reflection of the light of the SON. It is also symbolic of a woman, or the true church that is known as the bride of Christ. There is a religious system in the world that may call themselves Christians, but are governed by a spirit that is ruled by reason, logic, doctrine, and denomination. This may also be known as the Babylonian church (confusion) which is so prevalent in Christian circles today, represented by the many different denominations and doctrines.

The moon has no light of its own. In John's writing we have the moon under her feet. She is having a mountain top experience. No longer is the church/bride preparing herself to be the bride as the moon reflecting the Son, but she has now been a part of consummating the marriage as the wife carrying His seed.

This "woman" or "bride of Christ" comes to the conclusion that says, "Christianity is not about me, but about unifying the body of Christ through the mind of Jesus Christ." She has put the "moon" under her feet (Romans 16:20). Christianity is not about "self" getting into heaven, but awakening to the awareness that heaven is here and now in the midst of the world. An overcomer has the responsibility to intercede for others who are still in bondage of a religious system. They cannot go off and do their own thing because they don't want to be part of a religious system of doctrine and denomination. Those that have detached themselves from the body completely have simply formed another denomination and have created their own religion. An overcomer has the responsibility to "be in the world, but not of the world" being an intercessor for others as Jesus Christ did for each of us while we were in ignorance and darkness.

The crown with the twelve stars upon her head represents the government of God. It is a victor's wreath signifying a way of thinking and is symbolic of the mind of Christ ruling and reigning. Ask yourself, what is in your head? Do you think and respond the way Jesus would if he was in that same situation? We tend to forget that HE IS in that situation because we are in it, and because he is with us now and not sitting on a cloud somewhere. Jesus has already completed what was started from the beginning and has given all to the glory of the Father. Paul told the Colossians in 4:12 that, *"Epaphras, who is one of you, a servant of Christ, salutes you, always laboring* (interceding) *fervently for you in prayers, that ye may* (come to the understanding) *stand perfect and complete in all the will of God."*

God does not play a game of "chance" with us. Today we are complete and righteous in Him, however, the unveiling of our completeness is still in progress battling against our own logic and understanding.

David shares a song that we would do well to keep in our heart:
"The LORD will perfect that which concerns me; Your mercy, O LORD, endures forever"(Psalm 138:8 NKJV).

Whenever Scripture uses the words "may or might" in the translation consider taking out and reading it without these words. God does not do anything with "may or Might." His ways are perfect, complete, whole, and finished before time even existed. His ways are not dependent upon our "may or might." He chose us before the foundation of the world, and loves us despite the limitations we place upon ourselves and others.

What is it that concerns you? The Lord will reveal His perfection no matter what this concern is, allowing His mercy to endure forever, according to His good pleasure. So what is on the mind of this woman who wears a crown upon her head that has 12 stars? She has the mind of CHRIST; the mind of her husband, Jesus Christ, whom she knows intimately with an understanding of His unconditional love. She knows in her heart that *"as He is, so are we in this world"* (1 John 4:17). When diverse situations occur she hears her husband say, *"With men it is impossible, but not with God: for with God ALL things are possible"* (Mark 10:27).

Verse 2: *"And she being with child cried, travailing in birth, and pained to be delivered."*

If you were ever taught that the book of Revelation was for those that were left behind after a rapture of the church, this verse should bring questions in your heart. This woman is clothed with Christ and pregnant. Who is she? Everything is out of order in John's writings if we think it is the mother of Jesus which is how many theologians have taught.

This woman has been intimate with her husband and has His seed growing within her and she is ready to birth a son. Whenever a child is being born there is a lot of struggle for both the child and the mother. When God is dealing with us to come out of the Babylonian system there will be personal feelings that have to be cut off. At the birth of a child, there are two lives trying to survive; the mother and the child.

This woman is us with the revelation of our Heavenly inheritance now in the earth while in our natural body. To be the wife of Christ pregnant with the WORD of God being made flesh in our inner most being. (Psalm 138:1-2).

Verse 3: *"And there appeared another wonder in heaven; and behold a great red dragon, having seven heads and ten horns, and seven crowns upon his heads."*

Let us remember where John saw all of this taking place; he was in the Spirit on the Lord's Day. All of these symbolisms are spiritual things, not literal. He is on the Island Patmos known as "the place of my killing or death," and the only light he would be able to see in the darkest hour would come from the sky. I have literally been to the Island of Patmos and stood in the cave where John dwelt located at the high place of the Island. I was able to look out from the cave entrance and see the waters and small land mass of the ten-mile circumference of land. History tells us that John was not alone on the island, but with others that were abandoned to die in a place that offered very little food and water to survive, so there would have been an atmosphere of survival of the fitness that John, now an elderly man would have been dealing with. Once the night sky came upon him, he would have to be totally dependent on God to survive.

As he looks up to the stars there is a spiritual message. This "great red dragon" is also known by those that study the movements of the stars as "Draco" the dragon. Again, the stars are giving a message of spiritual understanding, not literal interpretation.

If we move ahead to verse 9 of this chapter, this red dragon is also referred to as: the old serpent, the dragon, the devil, and Satan. All of these names are about one thing; the thought process of humanity as separated from the mind of Christ.

Thoughts begin as seeds in in our spirit and soul. When we share them they become an ideal of potential, tangible reality in the earth. Thoughts are either from Christ or antichrist/ego. (Jeremiah 29:11).

The seven heads and ten horns and seven crowns upon his heads are not describing a literal monster, but are symbolic of the perfection, rulership, and complete authority of this creature. Who would this be? It is the first Adam.

The seven heads are symbolic of the fullness of the perfection of humanity. The ten horns refer to the law. All of this is spiritual bondage surrounded by death, incarceration, imprisonment, and captivity locked in human reason and logic. Adam was given complete rulership of everything through the ability to speak words. His source of creativity came from God (the Tree of Life) but he chose to challenge that source by eating from the Tree of the Knowledge of Good and Evil. This separated himself from his Father's wisdom until the time of Jesus.

In Genesis 3 we have a serpent in the Tree of Knowledge of Good and Evil. The word serpent in Hebrew is "nachash" which comes from the root meaning "to whisper," or to "hiss." The movement of a snake is difficult to interpret to avoid being bitten. When a thought has the intent of separation, division, self-focus, lust, greed, control, or power using divination mixed with the pure form of the Word of God, there is an antichrist/serpent spirit attached. This is not about awareness of what is happening in non-believers, but within the body of Christ. It is characteristic of the tribe of Dan which we will discuss shortly.

Paul was known as a rabbi in Biblical times of Jesus Christ. One of the first letters of correction he writes is to the Galatians. The territory where the Galatians resided was the ancient lands of the Celts who originated as the scattered northern tribes of Israel during the Babylonian captivity, then later scattered west towards the United Kingdom. They had lost their identity with the Torah blessings, yet still had rights to the birthright blessings of Abraham. The Jews referred to them as pagan gentiles because they were children of God full of mixture of the world without the teaching and instructions of the Father. Paul was addressing them as children of God, not pagan with the drawing of the Father's love to come back to their blessing rights through love and not by legalism allowing the Holy Spirit to be their teacher.

Inheriting the Kingdom of God is terminology Paul uses when writing to the Galatians of their birthright and blessing ability to bring Heaven into the earth through the body of Christ. He is not talking about a "lake of fire" or "going to hell."

Paul writes in Galatians Chapter Five the discernment of the fruit we eat and what tree is coming from. Many times the fruit of the Tree of Knowledge of Good and Evil will appear to be good, yet it will actually bring death. Paul says in Galatians 5:21-26, *"Envying, murders, drunkenness, reveling, and such like: of the which I tell you before, as I have also told you in time past, that they which do such things shall not inherit the kingdom of God. But the fruit of the Spirit is love, joy, peace, longsuffering, gentleness, goodness, faith, Meekness, temperance: against such there is no law. And they that are Christ's have crucified the flesh with the affections and lusts. If we live in the Spirit, let us also walk in the Spirit. Let us not be desirous of vain glory, provoking one another, envying one another."*

The 12 stars signify the finished work of the government of God that we are to manifest by coming through the 12 temple gates of pearl (Rev. 21:21). Pearls are formed by the transformation of sand inside an oyster. As the oyster tries to get the sand out, the pearl is formed and the animal dies. The number 12 takes us back to Genesis with the 12 sons of Jacob/Israel where the corporate body was first presented in scripture. Each son represents a portion of the different stages of growth and maturity we must go through spiritually as we come into our inheritance as a son of God. Remember, *"the earth is the LORD's, and everything in it, the world, and all who LIVE in it"* (Psalm 24:1 NIV). This is a promise for sons of God today, which we are not waiting until they get on the other side to receive their full inheritance.

In 1 Corinthians 3:16-17, Paul uses the imagery of the culture and the people's identification with the temple worship to redirect them sharing where the temple of God truly was. *"Know ye not that ye are the temple of God, and that the Spirit of God dwells in you? If any man defiles the temple of God, him shall God destroy; for the temple of God is holy, which temple ye are."*

At the time that John is writing Revelation, the temple in Jerusalem had fallen (70AD). John's writings date around 90AD. A new generation existed at this time, and era that was not familiar with the literal temple, yet they did have Paul's teaching (dated around 58AD) that references to the temple of God as the people, not a literal building.

Communications at this time in history was often done by symbols. The old literal temple had gates of entrances. Each gate had its own purpose of why a person would enter that particular gate. Again, the number 12 is symbolic of the government of God or the entrance into the city of God. It was identified by Jacob's 12 sons known as the Whole House of Israel. I realize that I have mentioned this several times, but if we only identify Israel with the tribe of Judah, then the church/the body of Christ cannot grasp the full understanding of their potential inheritance in the earth today.

Often times symbolism was used to help identify the individual tribes of Israel. These symbols would be placed on their banners, shields, and crests. As generations change with distance and time so did the variations of the symbols and emblems, however, they were still recognizable as keys to link the tribes together as they left the land of Israel and scattered among other nations. These emblems are found by Jacob's blessings to his sons in Genesis 49 and Moses identification of position each tribe would camp as they moved in one accord through the wilderness.

★ **Reuben** means "behold a son." This is the "new birth gate." We must be born again by coming to realize we are new creatures in Christ. Reuben was a first born that was unstable. He was identified by the waves of water. *"I am poured out like water, and all my bones are out of joint: my heart is like wax; it is melted in the midst of my bowels."* (Psalm 22:14)

★ **Simeon** means "hearing." This is the "hear the word of God gate." Faith comes by hearing the word speak to us personally. Simeon was identified by the sword as a watchman at the entrance. Are we hearing correctly?
"For the word of God is quick, and powerful, and sharper than any two edged sword, piercing even to the dividing asunder of soul and spirit, and of the joints and marrow, and is a discerner of the thoughts and intents of the heart." (Hebrew 4:12)

★ **Levi** means "union." We receive gifts from the Holy Spirit to bring us to the union gate. This gate brings us into full union and communion with all that God is. This is a oneness identity of the heart. Levi had no emblem, shield, or banner for his place was to attend the temple or body of Christ found in the other tribes.

★ **Judah** means "praise." This is the "true worship" gate. This gate is a praise and releasing of our life to worship God in Spirit and Truth. Judah was identified as a lion. Jesus was chosen to be birthed through this tribe to identify our position as the body of Christ. We not only must enter the gates with praise and thanksgiving, but in the midst of our trials and tribulations, we begin dealing with the challenges of the world with the joy of the Lord as our strength and armor. *"And now shall mine head be lifted up above mine enemies round about me: therefore, will I offer in his tabernacle sacrifices of joy; I will sing, yea, I will sing praises unto the Lord."* (Psalm 27:6)

★ **Zebulon** means "habitation." This gate is the "dwelling place." This is the place that we know we are in Christ and that Christ is in us. Zebulon's emblem was a ship with sails moving across water willing to be carried by the winds or the Holy Spirit as we habitat with Christ. Jesus demonstrated to His disciples the ability to walk on water. *"And Jesus said,*

Come. And when Peter was come down out of the ship, he walked on the water, to go to Him." (Matthew 14:29)

★ **Issachar** means "reward." This is the gate of "faithfulness." When we dwell with Christ we receive the reward of His peace, nature, identity. So often, this is where traditional interpretations of scripture end our Christian growth and maturity. This gate is not intended to be a place we enter after leaving our natural body. It is a stage of life we are meant to go through as new creations growing while we are on this earth as part of the maturing process. However, it is not the end of our maturation process; it is only half of the fullness that we are to receive. This tribe's emblem is a donkey carrying the sun, moon, and the stars. This tribe is identified with Bible scholars that desire the pure truth of the Word to become alive today. Mary rode into Bethlehem on a donkey, and Jesus rode into Jerusalem on a donkey. When Joseph had his dream in Genesis 37 we are informed that the Father is the sun, the mother is the moon, and the stars are our brothers and sisters in Christ. Through the pure form of the Torah we see Christ Jesus in all with the willingness to help carry one another's burdens without judgment. This is a hard thing to do! *"There is one glory of the sun, and another glory of the moon, and another glory of the stars: for one star differs from another star in glory.*" (1Corinthians 15:41)

★ **Dan** means "judge." This is the "judgment" gate. When we are in Christ we have the ability to judge righteously by seeing through the eyes of His righteous judgment of humanity. This tribe was identified by balanced scales, a serpent, and also a white horse. Justice and judgment comes in many forms of perception. This white horse was discussed in chapter 6. This is the appearance of Christ, but the heart of the antichrist. *"For as he thinks in his heart, so is he: Eat and drink, saith he to thee; but his heart is not with thee.*" (Proverbs 23:7)

★ **Gad** means "trouper." This is the "good fortune" gate. Our life in Christ is to be prosperous, not for ourselves, but so that we are able to bless others. We cannot give away what we don't have, so God will challenge us first to prove the condition of our hearts. What have we done with what He has already blessed us with? This tribe is symbolized with a troop of horsemen and/or a mounted leader of the troop. The discernment of our hearts has taken effect with judgment/justice and we have chosen to stay in unity with the body of Christ functioning together as one body. *"So we, being many, are one body in Christ, and every one members one of another."* (Romans 12:5), *"For we must all appear before the judgment seat of Christ; that every one may receive the things done in his body, according to that he hath done, whether it be good or bad."* (2 Corinthians 1:10), *"For as the body is one, and hath many members, and all the members of that one body, being many, are one body: so also is Christ."* (1 Corinthians 12:12).

> *As one body in Christ, what if we are judged before God by the negative deeds of our brothers and sisters in Christ, even though we didn't literally take part in them?*

★ **Asher** means "happy." This is the gate of "contentment." We come through this gate as we go beyond finding happiness and peace in things that they can see. We are now happy in the midst of trials. We have found His peace that surpasses all understanding. It is the joy of the Lord that gives us strength to overcome the challenges and hardships we are in. The emblems for this tribe are a royal goblet for wine and an olive tree branch. After trials and tribulations, there is an anointing and prosperity that has been yielded by the fruit of the vine through the blood of Jesus and the flowing of the Holy Spirit. *"Now will I sing to my well beloved a song of my* *beloved touching his vineyard. My well beloved hath a vineyard in a very fruitful hill"* (Isaiah 5:1)

★ **Naphtali** means "restlessness." This is the gate of "resting in the Lord." This gate must be entered after the other gates. If we go through this gate before any of the others, we will find ourselves wrestling with God instead of resting in His peace when trials come along. The emblem is a gazelle that has been set free from bondage to blessings of the Lord. *"The voice of my beloved! behold, he cometh leaping upon the mountains, skipping upon the hills."* (Song of Solomon 2:8)

★ **Joseph** means "abundant life" or "he will add life." This is the gate of "overflowing LIFE." The life of Christ is manifesting through us as we come through this gate. Our lives are now all about showing others their heavenly Father. We now have a heart cry that says, "Father forgive them for they no not what they do." Our one desire is to bring unity to the body of Christ through unconditional love and intercessory prayer. This gate is the way to the throne or mercy seat of God. This tribe carries several emblems that were divided between his two sons. He was identified as the fruitful branch of the olive tree along with arrows because of the many trials he endured through his life journey. Joseph's first born son, Manasseh, received these two emblems, the olive branch and the bundle of arrows.

> *The seal of the United States of America we see the olive branch and the bundle of arrows.*

Joseph was also identified by Moses as an ox/bull, a unicorn, and the horn. *"His glory is like the firstling of his bullock, and his horns are like the horns of unicorns: with them he shall push the people together to the ends of the earth"* (Deuteronomy 33:17). These emblems were given to his younger son Ephraim.

Ephraim was given a double blessing by his grandfather Jacob with an identification status change to sonship with his others sons. Ephraim was the only grandson to receive this blessing. Today we know that the Ephramites will be gathered together as the leaders in the body of Christ to re-unite the Whole House of Israel as one as prophesied by Ezekiel in chapter 37. They will lead with the anointing of Christ in them around the world blowing the horn of the unicorn, the voice of the Holy Spirit in them, into the world. The platform of the Father's grace will open the windows of heaven releasing His love, peace, and joy in the Holy Ghost into the earth reclaiming what the enemy had stolen. *"But go rather to the lost sheep of the house of Israel."* (Matthew 10:6).

★ **Benjamin** means "son of my right hand." This is the "son company" gate. When we come to this gate, we know the reality and full manifestation of being a son of God with all the power and authority we have in Christ Jesus. Our heart cry is "as He is, so am I in this world. I can do nothing except what my Father reveals to me." Paul tells us in Hebrews 6:1-3, *"Therefore let us leave the elementary teachings about Christ and go on to maturity, not laying again the foundation of repentance from acts that lead to death, and of faith in God, instruction about baptisms, the laying on of hands, the resurrection of the dead, and eternal judgment. And God permitting, we will do so"* (NIV).

The emblem for the tribe of Benjamin is the wolf. This tribe is often hidden by the dominance of the tribe of Judah sharing close territories. The lion comes across as the King, even among the animal kingdom, yet as we approach the Holy of Holies, the inner court sanctuary the wolf is seen as the guardian of the throne room of our heart. This is the place that separates the perception of what is LOVE? *"And the glory which thou gave me I have given them; that they may be one, even as we are one: I in them, and thou in me, that they may be made perfect in one; and that the world may know that thou hast sent me, and hast loved them, as thou hast loved me."* (John 17:22-23)

On a corporate/global level of the body of Christ, we can still see many of these tribal emblems identifying the whole house of Israel. In Jerusalem, Norway, Scandinavia, and North/West America we the symbol of the wolf. In Scotland, England, and the United States of America we see the olive branch and arrows. In Denmark, Netherlands, Scotland, and England we see the emblems of Ephraim. Many of the other tribal emblems can be found throughout Europe, Russian, the UK, and as far away as Australia.

> *There are a company of believers that have received the revelation knowledge that they were with Father God BEFORE they were conceived in the womb. They have been scattered to the nations and now long for the oneness with Him they knew before time.*

The prophesy in Ezekiel 37 states the Lord has promised that He will gather and regather the whole house of Israel together in a unity of oneness. Through the generations of intermarriages of tribes, people, language, and culture diversity there is no purity of a tribe. However, we will know the body of Christ by the emblems and the living stones each tribe was identified by on the High Priest breast plate, the heart of the Father. As the tribes are gathered together, the maturity as sons of God is manifested. From this we will begin to identify those that desire to prepare themselves as the bride. The Holy Spirit will identify them in their heart that they knew the beloved before time. (Jeremiah 1:5).

The Father draws those He has called though this gate. It is not a gate we can seek after, thinking it will make us more holy, but it is a place where we come to realize that we have the same heart as Jesus when he cried out to the Father, *"That they all may be one; as thou, Father, art in me, and I in thee, that they also may be one in us: that the world may believe that thou hast sent me. And the glory which thou gavest me I have given them; that they may be one, even as we are one: I in them, and thou in me, that they may be made perfect in one; and that the world may know that thou hast sent me, and hast loved them, as thou hast loved me"* (John 17:21-23).

Verse 4: *"And his tail drew the third part of the stars of heaven, and did cast them to the earth: and the dragon stood before the woman which was ready to be delivered, for to devour her child as soon as it was born."*

The tail belongs to the one called the "red dragon." In Isaiah 9:15 we read, *"the prophets who teach lies are the tail"* (NIV). This "dragon" is the thought process of carnal man. His use of logic and reasoning in understanding the word of God is built upon separation, judgment, and condemnation to the body of Christ. The mind of Jesus Christ is supposed to be controlling the tail; but instead, it still has the mind of the old Adam which speaks thoughts such as: "I am just a sinner saved by grace; I will never be good enough until I get to heaven; I am not worthy to be in the presence of God; O wretched man that I am." These thoughts will keep Christians in bondage so they will be unable to function in their true identities and unable to do the Father's business they were commissioned to do.

The dragon begins as a thought identified in the tribe of Dan with the law, the balance scales, the serpent in the Tree of Knowledge of Good and Evil, and the white horse of being a Christian with a strong ego as we discussed in chapter 6.

The tail, or false Christian mindset, drew a third part of the stars of heaven. The stars are the overcomers of the seed of Abraham. Remember the promise God made to Abraham in Genesis 15:5, *"Look up at the heavens and count the stars--if indeed you can count them." Then he said to him, "So shall your offspring be"* (NIV). The stars are symbolic of people. Abraham's seed was made of "dust, sand, and stars." These represented the three realms of the temple of God: outer court, middle court, and inner court or the Holy of Holies.

The star company are overcomers that strive to obtain the fullness of their inheritance while in their natural body for the purpose of uniting the body of Christ as one body. They understand that the position of sonship is a place of humble servant hood, not a place to use the power and authority they have to be seen as "holier than others." However, history has shown us that in less than a hundred years after the resurrection of Jesus, Christians began incorporating Greek mythology and Jewish legalism into the teachings of Jesus. He said in John 16:33, *"I have told you these things, so that in me you may have peace. In this world you will have trouble. But take heart! I have overcome the world"* (NIV).

Around 130AD a church Bishop named Marcion had great influence among new believers. Remember communication was limited, and illiteracy was common. The people relied that those with authority in the church were truly being honest. Marcion taught a strong belief in the Pauline doctrine focused from Luke and he encouraged a dismissal of the Torah and Old Testament, based on Paul's writings that said, *"For the law of the Spirit of life in Christ Jesus hath made me free from the law of sin and death"* (Romans 8:2). He took out of contents what Paul was sharing based on the teachings of Jesus when He said, *"Think not that I am come to destroy the law, or the prophets: I am not come to destroy, but to fulfil"* (Matthew 5:17). Jesus paid the penalty of sin which was keeping the children of God from an intimate relationship which could not be accomplished by the works of the Torah. The Torah was not to be thrown away, but unveiled through LOVE the blessings that are hidden for us to rule and reign as the Father's ambassadors in the earth.

Marcion was declared a heretic, but he still has a serpent's poison carried through church history that still is seen today in Bible translations, especially the Scofield Bible.

"And did cast them to the earth: and the dragon stood before the woman which was ready to be delivered, for to devour her child as soon as it was born." The word "before" literally means "in the face of." What are your eyes, your mind, and your heart looking at? Our thought processes will still deal with the 'dragon' that challenges our thoughts even though we

The tradition of this time period was the legal side of following the Torah. Paul taught the love language of the Torah unveiled through Jesus Christ, which is why he too was challenged as a heretic.

are the overcoming church (the woman). Even Jesus (the son of God) was confronted with trials and tribulations while ministering on the earth; especially in dealing with the religious leaders and their interpretation of the scriptures. The good news is that we are already victorious in Christ Jesus! Through Him, we truly can do all things to the praise and glory of God (Phil. 4:13)!

How often are we confronted with criticism once we receive a revelation from God that goes outside the box of current Christian teachings and are told "we have our doctrine wrong." In Paul's day those who went outside the box of traditional teachings were called "heretics." Remember, the label "Christian" was not a label Paul or the apostles placed upon themselves, but was a title given to them by those that did NOT believe. It wasn't until later that the name was used in a positive way to describe followers of Christ as one who had the identity and character of Jesus Christ.

What we call traditional Christian teachings today would not have caused an uproar among the gentiles and would not have brought Paul to martyrdom. The way Christianity at large portrays God today would have been accepted as similar in manner to the gods of the Greeks. The unique difference that caused the people to turn from their Greek mythology was that Paul revealed the resurrection power of Jesus Christ to the people. He didn't just talk about God identity as something that would occur someday when they would die. These people already believed they would be children of the god they worshipped when they left the natural realm. Part of their worship included picking out statues of what they wanted their bodies to look like after they died, and had a "bust" of themselves placed on this statue so that their families would have a visual of what they would look like in the afterlife as a "child" of the god they had been worshipping.

Paul preached that Jesus Christ is the Messiah, and the resurrection power in Christ Jesus is for NOW, not someday in the future. He preached the good news of the gospel of the Kingdom of God to both the Jews and the Gentiles that were living outside the land of Israel that we know today. His mission was to go after the lost sheep of the whole house of Israel. Many Gentiles did not know that they were descendent of Jacob, and many Jews were worshipping God by traditions of men. This is the message that challenged even the Gentile people to the point of wanting to persecute him. It is still the message most churches that call themselves Christian refuse to allow as truth because in doing so it would remove the control they have over the institution and the people. It is the same threat that existed between the Jewish leaders and Jesus. *"I want to know Christ and the power of his resurrection and the fellowship of sharing in his sufferings, becoming like him in his death, and so, somehow, to attain to the resurrection from the dead"* (Phil. 3:10-11, NIV).

Verse 5: *"And she brought forth a man child, who was to rule all nations with a rod of iron: and her child was caught up unto God, and to his throne."*

The words "man child" that are used to describe what has just come forth from a pregnancy comes from the word "huios" or a full-grown son. It is not the word "nepios" that would be used for an infant. The comprehension of this statement is enough to realize that we are not able to understand John's vision with literal comprehension.

It would be impossible in the natural for a woman to give birth to a full-grown adult.

The word "huios" (mature son) was used to clarify the message of the Holy Spirit revealed by John and is also the same word being revealed through Paul when he wrote in Romans 8:29, *"For whom he did foreknow, he also did predestinate to be conformed to the image of his Son, that he might be the firstborn among many brethren."* This man-child is the "word" in us; the DNA of Christ formed in Genesis 1:1-3 from the very beginning.

The WORD in us will rule all nations or anything that opposes God. The rod of iron is not a literal 'iron club' ready to strike when confronted with opposition, but symbolizes the uncompromising mind of Christ that mature sons of God manifest with their thoughts, character, and emotions. As mature sons, we will not be using scripture to justify what God says through carnal thoughts or reasoning.

> *The seed of God is the WORD. Christ is the Word, the Torah made flesh (John 1:14). Jesus is the head of Christ and the whole house of Israel is the body (Ephesians 4:15).*

Once the Holy Spirit has revealed our true identity in Christ, we will battle to cast down the imaginations once stirred by the old religious system of Christianity. These concepts and imagination will try to use reason and justification to take away the revelation given by the Holy Spirit.

God protects His seed and will bring the mature son to the throne or mercy seat of the Holy of Holies. God's word cannot be processed in a nursery school by those that have not been given the revelation. Only God can give the understanding and guidance of what is required in the Holy of Holies to mature sons of God. However, this is not a position of isolation where we separate ourselves from the body of Christ! It is a mindset of being a king and priest (maturity and intercession), that is full of mercy, forgiveness, and unconditional love to those that don't deserve it.

Paul tells us in Romans 8:1, *"There is therefore now no condemnation to them which are in Christ Jesus."* People that have not matured in Christ are like little children that need to be protected with the love of God by those that are walking in sonship. When we are living a life with the mind of Christ ruling us, we have the responsibility to be a king and priest to those that come across our path, utilizing the same wisdom and rulership that Jesus Christ revealed in our life for others. We are not to judge by sight, but by the Spirit of God.

Verse 6: *"And the woman fled into the wilderness, where she hath a place prepared of God that they should feed her there a thousand two hundred and threescore days."*

The corporate body of Christ Jesus is the whole house of Israel, all twelve tribes/that originated as sons of Jacob. The lost ten northern tribes that have been scattered to the nations around the world are being gathered together by the Spirit of God witnessing to their spirit that Jesus Christ is the Messiah and One God (Deut: 4:6). The church will desire to be taught the teachings of Moses, what is Holy and unholy, clean and unclean, and to honor the feast days of the Lord establishing the Kingdom of Heaven in the earth.

As we have discussed previously, the woman is the corporate body of Christ, the true church. Notice that

"And they shall teach my people the difference between the holy and profane, and cause them to discern between the unclean and the clean, and in controversy they shall stand in judgment; and they shall judge it according to My judgments: and they shall keep My laws/Torah and my statutes in all mine assemblies/church; and they shall hallow my Sabbaths." (Ezekiel 44:22-24).

God has prepared a place for the church. This is not a building we have labeled with a particular denomination. It is a corporate body of believers all around the world that are connected by the Spirit of God and His love. God has the corporate body of believers' right where they are supposed to be which is why those that are called into sonship must be careful not to be judgmental against the body of Christ. God is in control of everything! He is teaching us to listen to His voice to bring edification and love to the church from a higher level of understanding called: *intercession with unconditional love and forgiveness.*

Just as the natural lifecycle of humankind requires us to go through different stages of growth to obtain maturity; we are also required to go through this same process spiritually. We start off as children of God and mature into sons of God, and then prepare to be the bride of Christ as one body, not a lot of brides. There is only one body called the bride with many members. Her covenant with Jesus Christ is the Torah.

What we know as the church today, with its many different denominations, encourages growth and development but has been doing so at the level of teaching children. Maturity in Christ does not have to do with how long we have been a Christian, but by our faith in God that has been developed though trials and tribulations which gradually removes the "self focus" in each of us to becoming unified as one body in Christ. God uses the 'religious system' for training; but for maturing, He will send us each into the wilderness just as Jesus was sent in Matthew 4.

Jesus told His disciples that He would see them again after He had risen in the Galilee which was a three to four days' journey north of Jerusalem where they presently were. *"But after I am risen again, I will go before you into Galilee"* (Matthew 26:32). Jesus knew that the grip of fear would be so strong that they wouldn't be able to comprehend anything. He needed them to have a wilderness journey. After the resurrection, Jesus spoke several times to reinstate for the disciples to go to the Galilee where He would appear to them (Matthew 28:7, 10, 16).

This was all taking place during the Lord's feast of Passover, Unleavened Bread, and First Fruit. Most of Christians believe that the cross and resurrection is all the church is supposed to experience until the Lord returns. From First Fruit/Resurrection Day to Pentecost there is the longest feast day of the Lord called Counting the Omer. The Hebrew men were required by the Lord to appear in Jerusalem three times a year: Passover, Pentecost, and Tabernacles. Because of the difficulty in traveling as well as the observance of the Sabbath where there was no traveling, many men would have simply hung around the Jerusalem area for the next fifty days to be in Jerusalem for Pentecost. It would have been a challenge to consider walking to the Galilee and knowing they were supposed to turn around and come back to Jerusalem. The disciples needed the extra push to confirm they needed to go do to the fact that a spirit of fear was very strong in Jerusalem holding them captive and scared.

This journey they took to the Galilee would have followed the Jordan river where Jesus was baptized by John. They would have been reflecting the memories of what Jesus had shared and the miracles he did. This wilderness journey would have been in the same region that Jesus dwelled in for 40 days after he was baptized and then tempted by satan. Meeting Jesus in the Galilee AS THE RESURRECTION, then journeying with Him back to Jerusalem equipped the disciples to a greater understanding that "As He is, so are we today in this world" (1 John 4:17). As Jesus begins to prepare to ascend at the Mount of Olives, He tells them to tarry in Jerusalem until the Holy Spirit comes.

> *"To whom also he shewed himself alive after his passion by many infallible proofs, being seen of them forty days, and speaking of the things pertaining to the kingdom of God: And, being assembled together with them, commanded*

them that they should not depart from Jerusalem, but wait for the promise of the Father, which, saith he, ye have heard of me. For John truly baptized with water; but ye shall be baptized with the Holy Ghost not many days hence" (Acts 1:3-5).

The disciples waited in the upper room not having a clue of what it meant for the Holy Ghost to appear giving them power, yet there was an excitement in the atmosphere of faith instead of fear. They knew that Pentecost was in about ten days which was significant of Moses receiving the Torah from God. The Hebrew children saw this feast as a covenant commitment between God and His bride called a "Ketubah." If Jesus had done something miraculous at the Passover, unleavened bread, first fruits, and counting of the omer, they anticipated something to happen that had never happened before. In one accord they share their nuggets of memories, love, and life of Jesus singing praises on this very special day that the bride of Christ, the church is formed in the earth!

> *When the focus of being a Christian is to receive Jesus as our Lord and Savior, then tarry till we die and go to Heaven, we miss the blessings of the other Lord's Feast celebrations we were meant to enjoy in the earth.*

"They should feed her a thousand two hundred and three score days." The "they" in the wilderness are the sons of God, or the mature ones in Christ. These are people that will minister and intercede for us as we go through the trials of maturing. Their prayers are not a "hit or miss," but are sent with the absolute knowing of the mind of Christ, just as Jesus knew how to pray while on the earth. Matthew 4:11 tells us that "angels" came to minister to Jesus after the "devil" tempted him. These "angels" are messengers of God; or the cloud of witnesses that we have around us today.

The *"thousand two hundred and three score days"* is equivalent to three and a half years. This is symbolic of "ministry," not literally three and a half years. This is the amount of time that Jesus ministered on the earth. As I said earlier, there is a process of growth and development that each person is required to go through to become a son of God. Jesus' ministry involved the lives of twelve men and several women that were already children of God but were held in the captivity of religious bondage. Jesus ministered to them so that they would grow up in Christ for the purpose of doing the Father's business as He did. After Jesus ascended, the disciples were equipped to preach the good news of resurrection life found through Jesus Christ, who was now in them by the Holy Spirit. No other 'god' being worshipped at that time could heal the sick and raise the dead. This is why the message of the Gospel was so powerful and threatening to those who were in control of the pagan temples.

Verse 7: *"And there was war in heaven: Michael and his angels fought against the dragon; and the dragon fought and his angels,"*

The war in heaven is the war inside of us. The name "Michael" means "one who is like God." This is the Christ identity we each have. The "dragon" is our carnal reasoning that tries to bring logic into the realm of spiritual understanding. The word "against" is the word "midst." This war is between our ears, not somewhere outside of us or in another country.

> *Heaven is where God is. If Christ is in us there also is Heaven, the Kingdom of God at war with the "I AM" of Christ, and the I am of self.*

God uses external things to stir our internal spirit to clean out our natural understanding thus allowing His peace to surpass all logic and reasoning. Anything hidden in our heart must come out so that only God's presence will exist within us. He will not share His temple with anything: no fear, no frustrations, no condemnations, no anxieties, and no limitations. The only thing that must be left within us is His peace, and with that, we will be given the fruits of His Spirit (Galatians 5:22) so we can feed and encourage others.

While I was visiting the Island of Patmos in Greece, I was able to spend some time exploring the monastery's museum. There I saw a particular piece that looked like an ancient chandelier. I found it to be intriguing and was fortunate to have one of the monks explain the symbolism that surrounded it. The chandelier was made of silver covered in gold. It dated back to the early 2nd or 3rd century, and hung in the middle court of an Eastern Orthodox Church. At this time in history, the church was designed from the format of the Jewish temple (having outer, middle, and inner courts). Church hierarchies were established with priests likened to the Old Testament, but the people now had acceptance into the middle courts if they had been baptized. This monk explained to me that baptism to believers during this time in history was more than just symbolic to the public that they had received Jesus Christ as their personal savior. They believed they had literally experienced death and were now new creations in Christ; they knew that death would not be able to have an affect on them (body, soul, and spirit) from this point on, as long as they kept the faith as described in Paul's letters. However, they would experience temptation, which is where the chandelier comes into the picture.

The chandelier was huge with many places for candles to be placed. I would estimate it would hold at least 50 candles! It hung in the middle court. Each candleholder was created with beautiful designs of leaves and buds likened to flowers, but underneath each holder was the face of a dragon. The monk told me that dragons did not literally exist, but they were symbolic of man's creative power through imagination. The candleholder situated over the top of each dragon was symbolic of Christians being the light of the world as Jesus said in Matthew 5:14-16, "*Ye are the light of the world. A city that is set on a hill cannot be hid. Neither do men light a candle, and put it under a bushel, but on a candlestick; and it giveth light unto all that are in the house. Let your light so shine before men, that they may see your good works, and glorify your Father which is in heaven.*"

First, let's picture this chandelier hanging in a room full of people and being full of candles that were lit. The room was the sanctuary of the church so that when the Christians would come to worship they would look up at the chandelier and be reminded that "the dragon" or imagination had no power because they were now new creatures in Christ. Next, place yourself in a position higher than the chandelier, such as a second or third floor balcony, looking down upon it. In this position, since the room would be filled with light the people would not be seen. These people would be standing and singing praises to God (there was no room to sit down). Since they were baptized, they consider themselves as children of God literally, not just spiritually. You would not be able to distinguish any particular person below because the only thing noticeable would be the reflection of the light. This light would be extra powerful in this room because of the unique architect. Throughout the room there are gold icons and gold furnishings on the walls and furniture that would be reflecting the light from many different angles. Even the people in the room would have difficulty seeing the individuals around them because of the intensity of the light coming from the chandelier when all of the candles were completely lit.

Now this is the intriguing part about the chandelier when all of the candles were *not* lit. The people would not see light when they looked up, but the head of many dragons. They would not be any light coming from the reflective power of the gold that was surrounding them etched throughout the room, but would be sensitive to a dark, isolated environment that was cold and eerie.

If all of the candles in the chandelier were lit except one, there would be a sense of God's presence, but because the people could still see a faint image of the dragon's head from the *unlit* candle, they would not have the peace that surpasses all their body, soul, and spirit. It took ALL of the candles to be burning to have the room filled with the glory and presence of God, not only by what the candles created above, but by the reflection of the light that came from the gold in the furnishing in order for the people to experience total peace.

This chandelier was used during a time where communication was limited and most people did not read or write. They relied on visual understanding, which is why so many icons were created, not to be worshiped, but to tell the story of Jesus Christ. The people needed the visual presence of worship created in this room to release the peace in their hearts of knowing of their connection as brothers and sisters of a living Savior who conquered death, hell, and the grave. The illustration of the chandelier revealed to them that everyone's candle must be lit in order for the dragon's image to be removed. It took ALL of the candles on the chandelier to be lit in order to remove the ability to see the dragons.

The chandelier reminded them who they were in Christ, and it also reminded them of their ability to overcome death, hell, and the grave as Jesus did through the Holy Spirit. I also learned from the monk that this is the message that Paul, the Apostles, and John all preached and taught in the New Testament. Salvation has already been given to all at Calvary; however, to obtain the power of resurrection life it takes allowing the faith of Jesus Christ (given to each of us) to be released on a personal level. Not one Apostle experienced a natural death. They were all martyred except for John who did not die. It is believed by faith that he was transformed into the spiritual realm just as Moses, Enoch, and Elijah. Even many of the disciples of the Apostles had to be martyred because of the faith they too had in overcoming death. It wasn't until the third and fourth generations that the apostles' and their disciples' teachings began to be watered down and used to control and manipulate Christians with fear which we now know is in the realm of imagination.

To this day, those on the Island of Patmos consider there is a divine presence that death has been done away with because of the Apostle John never experiencing a physical death. Many of those that were born on the island have never left and have no desire to explore the other parts of the world. Many believe that they are as close to God as a person can obtain while on the earth which they would not be able to experience anywhere else. When I asked a native who was about 40 years old if he had any desire to even see the other islands or to go to the main land of Greece, he just said, "Why would I want to leave the presence of God here? I have everything I need here."

Today, we theorize a molecular level of transportation from place to another. Our Star Trek days of "beam me up Scotty" seems to extreme for our understanding. Yet, in the study of the mobile tabernacle of Moses in the wilderness, the magnetic energy created with the heat of the desert and the gold furnishings created a powerful electrical current that the priest would literally have to be transported to enter the idle and inner courts transforming their physical structure as if going through a solid object. It has taken over 2000 years since the time of Jesus to give thought to this potential that was already established during the times of Moses. What more does man have within our Christ anointing today that we have yet to unveil into the earth?

Verse 8: *"And prevailed not; neither was their place found any more in heaven."*

This is good news…knowing that God has already declared that there is no place for the enemy (dragon of our mind) in the spirit realm of His dwelling place. However, it takes coming into maturity as a son of God to be blessed with this understanding. Jesus said in John 8:37, *"I know you are Abraham's descendants. Yet you are ready to kill me, because you have no room for my word"* (NIV). Just because a person has received Jesus as their personal savior does not mean they have received the full understanding of their inheritance as a son of God. Many Christians do not have room in their hearts for the WORD, the teachings and instructions of the Father. Those that God has called into sonship understand that God does not share His temple with any other mindset. Only the mind of Christ can rule and reign with Jesus Christ in the house of God.

Verse 9: *"And the great dragon was cast out, that old serpent, called the Devil, and Satan, which deceiveth the whole world: he was cast out into the earth, and his angels were cast out with him."*

This is a verse that has been preached many ways over time by many preachers, usually from a perspective of creating a huge monstrous creature that looks like nothing ever seen on this earth, yet has been given so much power through the creative imagination of mankind that it thinks it can manipulate some of God's angels to follow it. Wrong, wrong, wrong! This dragon is not a literal creature, but the power of humanity's thinking process and his ability to create what he thinks. The tongue is the accomplice to in manifesting the power of the mind. I challenge you to search out the word "tongue" in a Bible concordance to see what scripture says about it. Here are just a few:

"They set their mouth against the heavens, and their tongue walketh through the earth" **(Psalms 73:9).**

"A wholesome tongue is a tree of life: but perverseness therein is a breach in the spirit" **(Proverbs 15:4).**

"Death and life are in the power of the tongue: and they that love it shall eat the fruit thereof" **(Proverbs 18:21).**

"Their tongue is as an arrow shot out; it speaketh deceit: one speaketh peaceably to his neighbor with his mouth, but in heart he layeth his wait" **(Jeremiah 9:8).**

"Even so the tongue is a little member, and boasteth great things. Behold, how great a matter a little fire kindleth! And the tongue is a fire, a world of iniquity: so is the tongue among our members, that it defileth the whole body, and setteth on fire the course of nature; and it is set on fire of hell. For

every kind of beasts, and of birds, and of serpents, and of things in the sea, is tamed, and hath been tamed of mankind: But the tongue can no man tame; it is an unruly evil, full of deadly poison" **(James 3:5-8).**

"Which deceived the whole earth." We are the sons of God manifested in an earthen creation by God. Deception came into our thinking process when the first Adam questioned his identity. Humankind has been searching for his identity over thousands of years and has finally come to the point of accepting the identity of the second Adam, Jesus Christ. Man now knows through the Word that, *"God is love. Whoever lives* (body, soul, and spirit identity) *in love* (unconditional) *lives in God, and God in him* (no duality in the mind and heart. Only the mind of Christ). *In this way, love is made complete* (total, finished, full inheritance) *among us so that we will have confidence on the day of judgment* (when our mind challenges us with "if you are a son of God") *because in this world we are like him. There is no fear* (anxiousness, confusion, duality of being a sinner) *in love. But perfect love drives out fear, because fear has to do with punishment. The one who fears is not made perfect in love* (not a son, but a child in training)" (1 John 4:16-18, NIV). When we know who we are in Christ we don't have to justify or prove our new identity to anyone. They will know we are Christ-ones by the love that flows through our hearts because they will hear the mind of Christ coming out of our mouths.

Verse 10: *"And I heard a loud voice saying in heaven, Now is come salvation, and strength, and the kingdom of our God, and the power of his Christ: for the accuser of our brethren is cast down, which accused them before our God day and night."*

This verse is full of the wisdom of who we are in Christ, but if we read it with our carnal understanding we will miss the blessing that it holds. Let's read it from another translation:

"And I heard a great voice in heaven, saying, Now is come the salvation, and the power, and the kingdom of our God, and the authority of his

Christ: for the accuser of our brethren is cast down, who accuseth them before our God day and night" (ASV).

This voice being heard in heaven is coming from within each one of us. Notice the word "now" is applied when the voice of God is heard. He doesn't say someday you will receive salvation, power, and the kingdom of God, but when you hear His voice. With the hearing we receive the authority of "his Christ." This is an interesting way of declaring the authority of God has been released. The word "his" signifies that the power and authority is not coming from someplace in the sky, but from within us to be released. We are kings, lords, and sons of God now. Once we hear the voice of our Father declaring that we are His beloved son in whom He is well pleased (because we are part of the body of Christ in whom Jesus Christ is the head) we instantly have the power and authority of the kingdom of God to cast down the accuser that has been in our head tormenting us day and night with thoughts of accusations, judgment, condemnation, and separation from the grace and mercy of God.

Jesus said to the people in John 12:32-36, *"And I, if I be lifted up from the earth, will draw ALL men unto myself. But this he said, signifying by what manner of death he should die. The multitude therefore answered him, We have heard out of the law that the Christ abideth forever: and how sayest thou, the Son of man must be lifted up? Who is this Son of man? Jesus therefore said unto them, yet a little while is the light among you. Walk while ye have the light, that darkness overtake you not: and he that walketh in the darkness knoweth not whither he goeth. While ye have the light, believe on the light, that ye may become sons of light. These things spake Jesus, and he departed and hid himself from them"* (ASV).

Jesus shared with the people that the accuser would be finished and no longer able to cause separation between God and humanity on the earth. The biggest lie that we have today in our Christian doctrine is that there is a place called eternal hell, and that God could be separated forever from humankind because of their unbelief. If this were true, then Jesus Christ did not finish the job of salvation, and He will never be able to have a perfect bride/body (Rev. 19:7). Salvation would not be a free gift based on God's unconditional love that endures forever, but a condition of law.

The word "hell" for the Hebrew mind originally meant separated from the Torah or the love relationship of the Father. It never meant an eternal place of torment. Many Christians today are living in hell because they do not believe they need the Old Testament.

Today, there is nothing more for Jesus to do. It is up to us as the body of Christ to grow up and mature into sonship by realizing that when Jesus died on the cross, we died also, and that when He arose from the grave, so did we. Today, as new creations in Christ (2 Corinthians 5:17), we have already been resurrected with Him and we have been given the power and authority of the kingdom of God to fulfill the law of love so that Christ will abide forever through the sons of God who have put all things under His feet (Hebrews 2:8).

The past two years, I've been trying to learn a few life lessons by growing a few grape vines. Not having a clue of what I was doing I accepted the challenge of planting two vines in good soil, and a sunny area. I also established a lattice for the vine to grow. It did well the first year, but only a few grapes. In Florida we don't have much of a winter season, so when all the leaves fell off and I just had a lot of barren vine, I thought they had died.

I started to pull the plants up and throw them away, but I never got around to it which was a good thing, because as soon as spring came out came lots of leaves. I fertilized and tried to train the vines, but they were going everywhere with small grapes that stayed hard, and just never fully ripened. I would trim back the vines to try and give the plants some kind of controlled shape, but that was as much as I was able to accomplish that year.

The leaves all fell off again and I'm back to the barren branches. Now that I can see more clearly what was underneath that tangled web of vines I decided to trim back all the little wild branches and stay focused on the main root branch. It took some time to make sure I was cutting back twigs and branches that were sucking the nutrition from the main branches. Many of these little branches had a curly vine as an anchor wrapped around the larger branches that made it challenging. I heard the Holy Spirit share with me the wisdom of what I was doing…

The history of Christianity has created wild branches that are so anchored in theology instead of Christ, that the vine, Jesus Christ in us, can produce very little quality fruit of the Holy Spirit in the earth. Each branch is more concerned with their own growth, their own church, that the body is not discerning His Body as one in the unity of faith. The body must be pruned back to the root foundation discerning the Lord's body. *"For those who eat and drink without discerning the body of Christ eat and drink judgment on themselves. That is why many among you are weak and sick, and a number of you have fallen asleep. But if we were more discerning with regard to ourselves, we would not come under such judgment"* (1Corinthians 11:29-31).

The best wine is made of grape clusters, not just one grape, that has been pressed, stomped, processed, and aged TOGETHER as one poured out wine, the blood of Jesus Christ. Selah!

Verse 11: *"And they overcame him by the blood of the Lamb, and by the word of their testimony; and they loved not their lives unto the death."*

Who was overcome? It is the accuser that is in our heads who has been named "Satan, the devil, the dragon, the antichrist, the evil one, etc." How was the accuser overcome? In Romans 5:8-9 Paul tells us, *"God commendeth his love toward us, in that, while we were yet sinners, Christ died for us. Much more then, being NOW justified by his blood, we shall be saved from wrath through him."*

The choice that all men are confronted with is not whether they are sinners (speaking of identity), but while they are in their natural body whether they want to live the life of God with all power and authority to do the Father's business. The other option is whether to live in doubt and insecurity that is tested by how "good" they are as a Christian.

Paul tells us that there is NOTHING that can separate us from our Father's love (Romans 8:39). God's love is not something that He has to make a choice about sharing, but it is the fullness of who He already is. We cannot separate ourselves from our Father no matter how much we may stumble in our thoughts and actions that do not line up with His character or nature. The trials of our hearts and minds are all part of the process that He created for us in order to grow up in Christ (James 1:2), so that His grace and mercy would be sufficient in all things.

In 2 Corinthians 12:7-10, Paul shares his personal difficulty with the voice in his head as he perseveres to be an overcomer for Christ; *"To keep me from becoming conceited because of these surpassingly great revelations, there was given me a thorn in my flesh, a messenger of Satan, to torment me. Three times I pleaded with the Lord to take it away from me. But he said to me, 'My grace is sufficient for you, for my power is made perfect in weakness.' Therefore I will boast all the more gladly about my weaknesses, so that Christ's power may rest on me. That is why, for Christ's sake, I delight in weaknesses, in insults, in hardships, in persecutions, in difficulties. For when I am weak, then I am strong"* (NIV).

"And by the word of their testimony; and they loved not their lives unto the death." The "word" IS the testimony of Christ that is IN US able to overcome the accuser in our head. This is the same experience Jesus was confronted with after the Father acknowledged that Jesus was His son. He was sent to the wilderness to cleanse any thoughts or ideas the accuser would challenge him with before he began doing the Father's business. Jesus overcame every temptation of mankind

for our sake. He paid the full price of all sin, or us missing the mark, that we were not able to fulfill on our own to come into the fullness of a relationship with our Heavenly Father.

These are overcomers that do not expect to receive the fullness of their identity someday when they die a natural death and go off someplace called heaven to be with the Lord. They have already put aside their natural understanding of where the kingdom of God is; giving no power to their soul that a literal death of the flesh is necessary to be with God. They are not going to someday be with the resurrected Jesus Christ, but consider themselves today as part of His resurrected body with His DNA, His power and authority, to overcome death, hell, and the grave. Not by anything that their natural mind can do, but because the life that is now being lived within them in the flesh is the life of Christ. Paul shared with the Galatians, *"If, while we seek to be justified in Christ, it becomes evident that we ourselves are sinners, does that mean that Christ promotes sin? Absolutely not! If I rebuild what I destroyed, I prove that I am a lawbreaker. For through the law I died to the law so that I might live for God. I HAVE* (it is already finished*) been crucified with Christ and I no longer live, but Christ lives in me. The life I live* (NOW) *in the body, I live by faith in the Son of God, who loved me and gave himself for me"* (Galatians 2:17-20, NIV).

> *"You, dear children, are from God and have overcome them, because the one who is in you is greater than the one who is in the world" (1 John 4:4).*

Verse 12: *"Therefore rejoice, ye heavens, and ye that dwell in them. Woe to the inhabiters of the earth and of the sea! for the devil is come down unto you, having great wrath, because he knoweth that he hath but a short time."*

The word "therefore" means "through this thing," and the word "rejoice" means "have a good frame of mind." James 1:2 says to, *"count it all joy when ye fall into divers temptations."* We should be reflecting the peace of God knowing that the accuser of the brethren has been cast down and there is no place for him in heaven, or within YOU!

"Woe to the inhabiters of the earth and sea." "Woe" means "pain, grief, and suffering." The devil can't touch those that know who they are in Christ as a son of God. However, those that are Christians waiting for their inheritance when they die "someday" are open invitations for the devil to cause chaos and havoc in their minds. Earth inhabiters would say, "I'm a sinner saved by grace, and need to crucify my flesh." They have an "outer court" or literal mentality of interpreting Scripture.

The inhabits of the sea are those that have entered into the middle court, or Holy Place. They have an understanding of the things of God through the revelation of the Holy Spirit, but they allow their carnal understanding (devil mentality) to enter this area also. They are the ones that are "casting off demons" or blaming the devil for the things

"So shall my word be that goeth forth out of my mouth: it shall not return unto me void, but it shall accomplish that which I please, and it shall prosper in the thing whereto I sent it" (Isaiah 55:11).

that occur. They are bringing "strange fire" into the Holy Place or the mind of Christ in them. They have the awareness of being transformed by the renewing of their mind, but they have yet taken the covenant vow on oneness with the Lamb.

Jesus said, *"Truly I tell you, if anyone says to this mountain, 'Go, throw yourself into the sea,' and does not doubt in their heart but believes that what they say will happen, it will be done for them"* (Mark 11:23). The mountain He is addressing is Mount Sinai, the Torah presented to the believers in Christ that were being tossed to and fro as a sea of people. Jesus is the Living Torah, the WORD made flesh. When we give people the true gospel of the Kingdom of God, not generations of man's theology, it will come to past.

When we come to the understanding of WHO WE ARE IN CHRIST there is no room for a devil. We realize that the real enemy of Christ is our own imagination and that we are dealing with the Battle of Armageddon in our head. The acknowledgment that I AM A SON OF GOD declares that the battle is finished and the devil (ego) must leave the body of Christ. Believe me, he does not go willingly, but will continue to challenge every cell of our body, soul, and spirit (likened to a cancer) until we know that we have been washed with the blood of the lamb, and know that we are the bride who has made herself ready…

"And I John saw the holy city, new Jerusalem, coming down from God out of heaven, prepared as a bride adorned for her husband. And I heard a great voice out of heaven saying, Behold, the tabernacle of God IS WITH MEN, and he will dwell with them, and they shall be his people, and God himself shall be with them, and be their God" (Rev. 21: 2-3).

Over two-thousand years ago, all of humanity was sealed in the tomb with Jesus. Three days later the stone was rolled away and Jesus came out as THE RESURRECTED LIFE. Today, we are all free. There is no death in the tomb, but the majority of people would rather stay shackled to the bondages of their imagination than leave the tomb behind to emerge as a new creature in Christ.

Verse 13: *"And when the dragon saw that he was cast unto the earth, he persecuted the woman which brought forth the man child."*

The word "saw" means "knew or knowing." Notice the persecution is to the woman, not the man-child. The reason is: when we accept who we are in Christ, our spirit identity cannot be touched or harmed. The challenge comes in the soulish realm in us also known as the woman. Today, we are no longer "living souls" as the first Adam, but "life-giving spirits" as the second Adam, Jesus Christ (1 Corinthians 15:45).

Verse 14: *"And to the woman were given two wings of a great eagle, that she might fly into the wilderness, into her place, where she is nourished for a time, and times, and half a time, from the face of the serpent"*

"Given two wings of a great eagle" is likened to our soul (the woman or individual person) being given divine protection for the purpose of God being fulfilled while in our natural body. Each one of us are here on this earth for a reason. God has a purpose for the organized church system (the corporate body of Christ) and He has given her (woman) divine protection from the face, or identity of the serpent, the accuser of the brethren, which is the mind of humanity.

The Christian church has gone through many generations of turmoil as the innocence and ignorance of believers left themselves bound and controlled by those who manipulated the scriptures. Yet, in every generation God has equipped a company of believers to carry the seed of His divine truth of unconditional love, peace, and mercy into the next generation. The Holy Spirit gave John graphic physical imagery to help us understand spiritual wisdom.

Jesus Christ is the head of the body, but he is not independent to Himself. The head is dependent upon the body to respond to the impulses of the mind of Christ, which are sent by the Holy Spirit. The return of Jesus demands a body that the LIFE of Christ flowing through it from the head down to every cell, where the scripture is fulfilled that every knee shall bow and every tongue confess that Jesus Christ is Lord (Romans 14:11, Phil. 2:10). This fulfillment is not a someday when we get to heaven, but a seed fact that Jesus Christ instilled into every person when He declared "it is finished" (John 19:30). He bowed His head and gave up the Holy Spirit to be released to the body so that when He was seen again by the disciples after the resurrection He was no longer ministering to men, but brothers and sisters in Christ.

"Then said Jesus to them again, Peace be unto you: as my Father hath sent me, even so send I you. And when he had said this, he breathed on them, and saith unto them, receive ye the Holy Ghost: Whose soever sins ye remit, they are remitted unto them; and whose soever sins ye retain, they are retained" (John 20:21-23). With these words, Jesus declared that "ye are gods" of your Heavenly Father whom you know as God (John 10;34).

Remember the story of Jesus healing the man with palsy in Mark 2:5-12? *"When Jesus saw their faith, he said unto the sick of the palsy, Son, thy sins be forgiven thee. But there were certain of the scribes sitting there, and reasoning in their hearts, why doth this man thus speak blasphemies? WHO CAN FORGIVE SINS BUT GOD ALONE? And immediately when Jesus perceived in his spirit that they so reasoned within themselves, he said unto them, Why reason ye these things in your hearts? Whether is it easier to say to the sick of the palsy, Thy sins be forgiven thee; or to say, Arise, and take up thy bed, and walk? But that YE MAY KNOW THAT THE SON OF MAN HAS POWER ON EARTH TO FORGIVE SIN, (he saith to the sick of the palsy,) I say unto thee, Arise, and take up thy bed, and go thy way into thine house. And immediately he arose, took up the bed, and went forth before them all; insomuch that they were all amazed, and glorified God, saying, We never saw it on this fashion."*

The ability for us today to forgive one another unconditionally was not part of the culture during the time of Jesus. Only those of the Levite tribe had any ability to extend forgiveness to the people. The fact that we can forgive unconditionally is the inheritance given to us by God through Jesus Christ (since it is now our nature in Him to forgive).

As children of God we each have a ministry established by our Heavenly Father to unite the body of Christ together in His identity, character, and nature. We are protected by the Holy Spirit, just as Jesus demonstrated while on the earth, that the face of the serpent, or the logic and reasoning of humanity, will not be able to hinder the divine calling on our life.

Verse 15: *"And the serpent cast out of his mouth water as a flood after the woman, that he might cause her to be carried away of the flood."*

What is coming at the woman (our soul) are worldly words such as, "Who do you think you are? How dare you compare yourself to the Son of God! How dare you think you can be part of God!" Remember, the enemy knows God, but he also knows your insecurities. Let's go back to Genesis to refresh our memories of the conversation that the WOMAN had with the serpent (accuser):

"Now the serpent (mind of man) *was more subtle than any beast of the field which the LORD God had made. And he said unto the woman* (his soul), *Yea, hath God said, Ye shall not eat of every tree of the garden? And the woman* (soul, logic, reasoning) *said unto the serpent* (accuser in the mind of Adam), *We may eat of the fruit of the trees of the garden: But of the fruit of the tree which is in the midst of the garden* (Yes, but God did not tell Adam he couldn't eat of the tree of Life which was also in the midst), *God hath said, Ye shall not eat of it, neither shall ye touch it* (God did not say the word "touch." This was added by Adam's logic and reasoning of the senses), *lest ye die. And the serpent said unto the woman, Ye shall not surely die: For God doth know that in the day ye eat thereof, then your eyes shall be opened, and ye shall be as gods, knowing good and evil"* (Genesis 3:1-5). This last statement was a partial 'truth' given by the accuser through logic and reasoning of the senses that Adam introduced with the word "touch." The man and the woman were already children of the most High God, they were gods of LIFE and LOVE; however, by eating from the Tree of Knowledge of Good and Evil, they became gods of reason and logic. They knew right and wrong (which placed their senses in control of LIFE) but they didn't know their oneness with the Life-giver Himself.

Unfortunately, we still find the accuser of the brethren (the serpent) trying to subtly use the Scriptures (the water) to control and manipulate the body of Christ through legalism, doctrines, and traditions. The church has been bombarded with bondages that have caused separation and division in the body of Christ. In order to break free from these bondages of control, the church must realize who she is as the body of God (Jesus Christ). Since we know the finished work of Jesus Christ, we know that *"as He is, so are we in this world"* (1 John 4:17), and that it is God's divine will that He is all and in all (1 Corinthians 15: 28).

Verse 16: *"And the earth helped the woman, and the earth opened her mouth, and swallowed up the flood which the dragon cast out of his mouth."*

The words "her mouth" is referring to the first two realms of the temple of God (outer and middle courts, also known as the dust and sand companies). So, even though "the church" is operating in a carnal way apart from faith, God will still use this system to protect the woman; or those who carry the seed of the revelation of sonship. This is one of the many reasons why we cannot separate ourselves from the rest of the body of Christ. Another reason is so that we can show by example the now reality of the kingdom of God. Those that consider themselves Christians and believe that heaven is a "someday" destination will be challenged to grow up into the maturity of knowing heaven on earth in Christ Jesus. Their first response will be to justify that they are right in their interpretation of scripture regarding the someday realities of heaven versus the kingdom as already here. They will try to separate themselves, but the fact that they declare themselves Christians will go against their ability to exclude you. For them to stay in the presence of an "overcomer," they will be tormented in their heart and mind until the unconditional love of God overcomes their natural reasoning.

Verse 17: *"And the dragon was wroth with the woman, and went to make war with the remnant of her seed, which keep the commandments of God, and have the testimony of Jesus Christ."*

The word "wroth" is "enraged." The "dragon" or "carnal mind" will be frustrated because it is not able to reason with the person that is declaring their identity as a son of God. Since there is nothing the carnal mind can do to harm this identity, the carnal mind will try to go after the seed by questioning "if you are the son of God, then prove it! Why don't you heal yourself, or remove yourself from being crucified and tormented?" A son of God knows that their life is hid in Christ. They have been crucified in HIM, and the life they now live is not about "what's in it for themselves," but for the unity of one body in Christ to be manifested on this earth. The earth belongs to God and the fullness of it. While most of the church is yearning to someday escape to a far away place they call heaven, all of creation has been groaning for the manifestation of the sons of God.

Paul presents this to us in Romans 8:19-23 where we read, *"For the earnest expectation of the creation eagerly waits for the revealing of the sons of God. For the creation was subjected to futility, not willingly, but because of Him who subjected it in hope; because the creation itself also will be delivered from the bondage of corruption into the glorious liberty of the children of God. For we know that the whole creation groans and labors with birth pangs together until now. Not only that, but we also who have the firstfruits of the Spirit, even we ourselves groan within ourselves, eagerly waiting for the adoption, the redemption of our body"* (NKJV).

Jesus did not come to do away with the Torah, the prophets, and the writings of the Old Testament, but fulfill the penalty of sin and death so that we could enter into the blessing of the teaching and instructions of the Father (Matt. 5:17).

Having an understanding of the commandments of God requires more than just knowing the ten commandments or the rules established by the Levitical Priesthood. The commandments of God are found in the Torah from Genesis to Deuteronomy. Jesus did not come to remove these commandments, statues, and judgments but He did fulfill them by releasing God's unconditional love, forgiveness, and mercy in the earth. Jesus did not come to do away with the Torah, the prophets, and the writings of the Old Testament, but fulfill the penalty of sin and death so that we could enter into the blessing of the teaching and instructions of the Father (Matt. 5:17). Without this foundation of God's identity and character in us, we cannot BE sons of God, but will wonder as children to and fro.

Jesus gives us an example of child-like versus mature son behavior in Matthew 15:4-9, *"For God commanded, saying, Honor thy father and mother: and, He that curseth father or mother, let him die the death. But ye say, whosoever shall say to his father or his mother, it is a gift, by whatsoever thou mightest be profited by me; And honor not his father or his mother, he shall be free. Thus have ye made the commandment of God of none effect by your tradition. Ye hypocrites, well did Esaias prophesy of you, saying, this people draweth nigh unto me with their mouth, and honoureth me with their lips; but their heart is far from me. But in vain they do worship me, teaching for doctrines the commandments of men."*

Sonship is not about doing something, but about BEING in Christ, which takes the faith of God to believe.

"If ye then be risen with Christ, seek those things which are above, where Christ sitteth on the right hand of God. Set your affection on things above, not on things on the earth. For ye are dead, and your life is hid with Christ in God" (Colossians 3:1-3).

Notes of Reflection

What were your immediate thoughts in this chapter?

_____

_____

_____

_____

_____

What preconceived thoughts did you have before reading this chapter?

_____

_____

_____

_____

_____

What new information did you learn?

_____

_____

_____

_____

_____

Does this information seem confusing or liberating? Why?

_____

_____

_____

_____

_____

CHAPTER 13

The Beast

"And I stood upon the sand of the sea, and saw a beast rise up out of the sea, having seven heads and ten horns, and upon his horns ten crowns, and upon his heads the name of blasphemy"

As we begin with verse one in this chapter, let us remember what the Book of Revelation is about: THE REVELATION OF JESUS CHRIST (within you). John is not writing about something that is going to happen externally, but about Christ who has come to live within His people (to indwell in His temple). The imagery that was given to John by the Holy Spirit illustrates the transformation that takes place individually, then corporately, as the body of Christ is united and ruled with the mind of Christ. It is by this progression of transformation that Jesus Christ, who is the head of the body, will return in the fullness of His glory. The message throughout this book is not to be measured by what we do, but by who we are in Christ. When we live out the reality of our union with Christ, we will change the atmosphere around us. By renewing our minds to this union, we will outwardly manifest Christ's nature.

Verse One: John is not literally standing upon the sand of the sea. This is an allegory symbolizing spiritual truth that is connected to what John wrote in chapters 11 and 12 about the 7th or last trumpet.

Remember that in chapter four John was told to "come up here" into the heavenly realm of understanding. He is still there (spiritually) in the presence of God (seated with Him). From this position on the mercy seat looking back toward the Holy Place and outer court, there is no veil separating the inner court from the other courts. It was destroyed at Calvary. John is witnessing the spiritual understanding of the people in the middle or Holy Place while being spiritually seated in heaven with Jesus Christ. In order to sit on the mercy seat of God we must know who we are in Christ. It takes knowing that we are kings and lords of THE KING AND LORD.

Notice that John is using the word "beast" and not the name of a particular animal like a gorilla or bear. Webster's dictionary describes the word "beast" as a despicable, contemptible person. This "beast" is man's "ego" arrayed in his own glory (Ezekiel 28). These are Christians (not non-believers) that are likened to wolves in sheep's clothing that use the word of God to justify their "good" behavior and their "right" to point a finger at the faults of others. They focus on how to be "good Christians" and are motivated by the rewards they will receive in heaven, but their judgments cause separation and division in the body of Christ.

> *"And I will call for a sword against him throughout all my mountains, saith the Lord GOD: every man's sword shall be against his brother" (Ezekiel 38:21).*

The problem many people have with chapter 13 is a misunderstanding of the "mark of the beast." It has been taught by theologians as something stamped in our foreheads or forearms by the antichrist that could keep us from entering heaven. For centuries people have feared several different things out of ignorance about what this mark really is. In reality, everyone has already been subjected to the "mark of the beast" because of Adam's sin, which caused humanity to fall short of their true identity in Christ. This mark has existed since the fall of Adam in Genesis chapter 3. However, the power it possessed was destroyed at Calvary. Any power it may seem to have today is only because of the fear, ignorance, and insecurity man has allowed himself to create with his imagination.

When we started our study of the Book of Revelation, we read in the first chapter, verses 5 and 6 that it is, *"Jesus Christ, who is the faithful witness, and the first begotten of the dead, and the prince of the kings of the earth. Unto him that loved us, and washed us from our sins in his own blood, and hath made us kings and priests unto God and his Father; to him be glory and dominion for ever and ever. Amen."* Jesus Christ is the faithful witness who removed and destroyed everything pertaining to this "mark" when he died at Calvary and was resurrected from the dead as the first begotten son.

Our salvation is not based by whether or not our flesh has been stamped or tattooed with a "666" mark. We have already been saved spiritually through Jesus Christ who died once and for all. It is our souls that must be awakened to our true nature and identity in Christ. What is "stamped" on our heads or hands is symbolic of what we are thinking and doing.

This "beast" is not a mature believer in Christ, but someone who has some understanding of the Scriptures and of what it means to be a Christian; however, the authority given to them by the Holy Spirit to function as kings and priests is not being used to unite the body of Christ in love, but to bring judgment and condemnation to those around them. They are not intentionally vindictive, but the imagination or the beast within their head is battling with TRUTH.

The "seven heads" symbolizes the perfection we have in spirit. However, even though God has declared our perfection in Him, we must go through trials and testing periods in our life with what is in our head lining up with our heart – God's throne room - to bring the soul and body into that perfection. Every time the word of God rises up within us, a battle will take place against our carnal understanding as it tries to justify and control our spiritual (Christ) identity. This is why John uses the word "beast." King David declares in Psalm 73:22, *"So foolish was I, and ignorant: I was as a beast before thee."*

In Proverb 9:1-2 we read, *"Wisdom hath builded her house, she hath hewn out her seven pillars: She hath killed her beasts; she hath mingled her wine; she hath also furnished her table."*

God says we are perfect (Phil. 3:15) with the mind of Christ today (1 Cor. 2:16). We cannot replace God with our own perfection; however, we are each in Him as part of His body with His DNA or "seed identity." Even though Scripture says we are perfect now, most Christians believe that we cannot come into perfection until after we die. So while we are still in our natural body, the law has been mixed with grace to control our imperfections created by our imagination pictured here as "ten horns." Our perfection is to be manifested by the faith of God in us, not by the bondages of "being a Christian." Let's read what Paul wrote to the Galatians in 2:17-3:3:

> *"But if, while we seek to be justified by Christ, we ourselves also are found sinners, is therefore Christ the minister of sin? God forbid. For if I build again the things which I destroyed, I make myself a transgressor. For I through the law am dead to the law, that I might live unto God. I am crucified with Christ: nevertheless I live; yet not I, but Christ liveth in me: and the life which I now live in the flesh I live by the faith of the Son of God, who loved me, and gave himself for me. I do not frustrate the grace of God: for if righteousness come by the law, then Christ is dead in vain. O foolish Galatians, who hath bewitched you, that ye should not obey the truth, before whose eyes Jesus Christ hath been evidently set forth, crucified among you? This only would I learn of you, Received ye the Spirit by the works of the law, or by the hearing of faith? Are ye*

so foolish? having begun in the Spirit, are ye now made perfect by the flesh?"

Today, we have already been circumcised and cleansed from what used to be the source of our spiritual life, the old Adam nature. *"Beware lest any man spoil you through philosophy and vain deceit, after the tradition of men, after the rudiments of the world, and not after Christ. For in him dwelleth all the fullness of the Godhead bodily. And ye are complete in him, which is the head of all principality and power"* (Colossians 2:8-10). If we do not believe that we are NOW sons of God, it is because we have allowed "the beast" to rise up and suppress our true identity in Christ.

The "ten horns" or the law is found today in Christian doctrines, formulas, routines, regiments, boundaries, limitations, and traditions. These things cause man to look at the external issues. The only boundary we should be concerned with is the love in our hearts; the law has been fulfilled. When a lawyer challenged Jesus by asking which was the greatest commandment of God, Jesus answered, *"Thou shalt love the Lord thy God with all thy heart, and with all thy soul, and with all thy strength, and with all thy mind; and thy neighbor as thyself"* (Luke 10:27).

In Hebrew terminology, numbers carry a deep meaning than just a numeric value. The number ten can be written as "10", but it can also mean "1+0=1", or "1x0=0". It is a number that signifies a new level of what is already established. The number "1" is always identified with YHVH, one God. The number "0" is identified with eternal, alpha/omega, beginning and end.

The most familiar principle Christians identify with the number ten would be the ten commandments or the ten plagues of Egypt. In Hebrew these are the principles, statues, and judgments of God. There is an atmospheric sound heard referred to as horns as a shofar or the voice of the commandments. Before Jesus Christ came to the earth this was identified as the law to keeping a relationship with God. The law of sin and death was done away with after the resurrection opening up the veil of the Holy of Holies to enter into the presence of the Father through the love of God released to us through Jesus Christ. It is now permissible to receive the instructions of the Father as His blessings to His children while on the earth instead of waiting till we die and cross over to the other side. The commandments are not our means of Salvation, but our blessings of the Kingdom of God in the earth.

The only law we should have is to love...not only by what we say, but also by what we do (1 John 3:18). As sons of God, we have been given the position of authority to see others from the position of their righteousness in Christ. We have the capability to look at their hearts and not their external actions. With the love of God, we also have the ability to see strangers as brothers and sisters in Christ even though they do not acknowledge that we are all part of the family of God.

As we finish up with verse one we read *"and upon these ten horns were ten crowns, and upon his head is the name of blasphemy."* These crowns symbolize the rulership that is connected with the law. This is not the law of love, but it comes from the "beast" of natural man found in those that call themselves Christians. Remember that the "sea" is symbolic of believers in Christ who have entered into the middle court. They may be known as being spirit-filled, Pentecostals, or the Charismatic movement. I appreciate this time of growth that is necessary for the body of Christ, but my experience with those in this stage of development is the manifestation of separation and confusion to the body instead of love and unity. Many

A spirit of Confusion in the church is like trying to move forward with a vision, but it is necessary to crossover through muddy waters. You don't know how deep, or how dangerous those waters might be, and you don't know what beast may be hidden in them.

Christians consider that they have the fullness of power and authority at this stage forgetting that there is a Tabernacle experience we all must go through to be seated in heavenly places (the mercy seat of God). Paul tells us, *"Let no corrupt communication proceed out of your mouth, but that which is good to the use of edifying, that it may minister grace unto the hearers. And grieve not the Holy Spirit of God, whereby ye are sealed unto the day of redemption"* (Ephesians 4:29-30).

The "name of blasphemy" is not literally referring to someone with this name, but having this imagination, which speaks against the nature and character of God, yet they believe they are acting as a Christian. Paul sums up this verse in Galatians 5:13-6:2:

> *"You, my brothers, were called to be free. But do not use your freedom to indulge the sinful nature; rather, serve one another in love. The entire law is summed up in a single command: "Love your neighbor as yourself." If you keep on biting and devouring each other, watch out or you will be destroyed by each other. So I say, live by the Spirit, and you will not gratify the desires of the sinful nature. For the sinful nature desires what is contrary to the Spirit, and the Spirit what is contrary to the sinful nature. They are in conflict with each other, so that you do not do what you want. But if you are led by the Spirit, you are not under law. The acts* (which begins in the mind with words of imagination) *of the sinful nature are obvious: sexual immorality, impurity and debauchery; idolatry and witchcraft; hatred, discord, jealousy, fits of rage, selfish ambition, dissensions, factions and envy; drunkenness, orgies, and the like. I warn you, as I did before, that those who live like this will not inherit the kingdom of God* (righteousness, peace, and joy in the Holy Ghost). *But the fruit of the Spirit is love, joy, peace, patience, kindness, goodness, faithfulness, gentleness and self-control. Against such things there is no law. Those who belong* (know who

they are as a son of God) *to Christ Jesus have crucified the sinful nature with its passions and desires. Since we live by the Spirit* (mind of Christ), *let us keep in step with the Spirit. Let us not become conceited, provoking and envying each other. Brothers, if someone is caught in a sin, you who are spiritual* (cover him with the love of Christ through intercession for the body of Christ) *should restore him gently. But watch yourself, or you also may be tempted. Carry each other's burdens, and in this way you will fulfill the law of Christ"* (NIV).

Verse 2: *"And the beast which I saw was like unto a leopard, and his feet were as the feet of a bear, and his mouth as the mouth of a lion: and the dragon gave him his power, and his seat, and great authority."*

Notice that John uses the word "like" to describe "the beast." If we would allow the Bible to interpret itself we would find this same imagery used by Daniel in chapter 7. If there were any literal understanding about this imagery, it would have already happened before Jesus Christ walked the earth.

In Daniel 7:2 he writes about four winds, which we also find in Zechariah as four horses or in the New Testament as the four gospels. The winds spread the gospel, and the messenger becomes one with the message. Daniel tells us that the beast does not come out until the winds begin to blow. The Holy Spirit will reveal Christ in each of us, but He will also expose what is not Christ; not in a judgmental condemning way, but as purification surrounded by love which causes us to question, "if this truly is Christ, then what have I been taught?"

> *"Daniel spoke and said, I saw in my vision by night, and, behold, the four winds of the heaven strove upon the great sea" (Daniel 7:2)*

Again, these are not literal beastly creatures that John is writing about. This is not a literal leopard that really has bear's feet and a lion's mouth. We are talking about the character and nature of believers in Christ who are still living under the laws of carnal man. The unique characteristic about a leopard is that it has spots. Ephesians 5:26-27 tells us, "*That he* (the spirit of God in us) *might sanctify and cleanse it* (any opposition to God) *with the washing of water by the word, that he might present it to himself a glorious church, not having spot, or wrinkle, or any such thing; but that it should be holy and without blemish.*"

God does not see any flaws in us today. He made us perfect in the day that we were created, and He does not make any mistakes. God knew us before the foundations, before we were conceived. It is our own imaginations, thoughts, and actions that must be adjusted to line up with who the word says we are. We have to get beyond the dust and sand mentality (outer and middle court) and come into the star company (inner court) where we are seated today in heavenly places (understanding).

"My frame was not hidden from you when I was made in the secret place, when I was woven together in the depths of the earth. Your eyes saw my unformed body; all the days ordained for me were written in your book (Torah) before one of them came to be. How precious to me are your thoughts, God" (Psalm 139:15-17)

The "bear" represents the deep, heavy and intense obstacles in our lives (all the things which need to be put under his feet) Ephesians 1:22. God's kingdom has no discord or problems. We lack the manifestation of the power and harmony of the Kingdom of God because we do not seek the inner knowledge of who we are in Christ.

The "lion" is symbolic of the king of all creatures. It represents those that are believers in Christ. Jesus Christ is the King of kings. The problem with this picture is that instead of their words edifying and bringing unity to the body of Christ in

> *"The scepter will not depart from Judah, nor the ruler's staff from between his feet, until he to whom it belongs shall come and the obedience of the nations shall be his" (Genesis 49:10).*

the Father's love, they roar with judgment and condemnation (spots of a leopard and obstacles of a bear). The lion represents the tribe of Judah; the tribe that Jesus was brought from heaven into the earth. The tribe of Judah carries the scepter that leads the army of God into battle with the victory cry and the sound of praises unto God.

There is another lion in scripture that Peter reminds us of known as the devil, the accuser of the brethren who roams around as a lion to devour. *"Be alert and of sober mind. Your enemy the devil prowls around like a roaring lion looking for someone to devour"* (1 Peter 5:8). These are Christians that are kings and lords of the Kingdom of Jesus Christ, but they separate and divide the kingdom instead of unite as one body in Christ Jesus.

Let's read what Jesus says in **Matthew 15:6-20:**

> *"You hypocrites! Isaiah was right when he prophesied about you: These people honor me with their lips, but their hearts are far from me. They worship me in vain; their teachings are but rules taught by men." Jesus called the crowd to him and said, "listen and understand. What goes into a man's mouth does not make him 'unclean,' but what comes out of his mouth, that is what makes him 'unclean.'" Then the disciples came to him and asked, "Do you know that the Pharisees were offended when they heard this?" He replied, "Every plant that my heavenly Father has not*

planted will be pulled up by the roots. Leave them; they are blind guides. If a blind man leads a blind man, both will fall into a pit." Peter said, "Explain the parable to us." "Are you still so dull?" Jesus asked them. "Don't you see that whatever enters the mouth goes into the stomach and then out of the body? But the things that come out of the mouth come from the heart, and these make a man 'unclean.' For out of the heart come evil thoughts, murder, adultery, sexual immorality, theft, false testimony, slander. These are what make a man 'unclean'; but eating with unwashed hands does not make him 'unclean'" (NIV).

In finishing this verse, we see the dragon connected with the leopard, bear, and lion symbolism. I find it humorous to think that if we were confronted with these animals in a natural habitat a "dragon" would ever give its position over to these other animals. If we would just stop and think, we would see that John was prophesying metaphorically with parables. As we mentioned earlier, the dragon is the "imagination created by self or carnal mind" which challenges the mind of Christ within you. The dragon image began as a thought, a serpent's heart that asks, "Did God say that? If you are who you say you are, then? Don't you remember the bad things you did? Your visions are impossible!"

Paul battled with this atmosphere in his travels. *"Let the communication of your faith become effectual by the acknowledging of every good thing which is in you in Christ Jesus"* (Philemon 6); *"for it is Christ that is in you, the hope of glory"* (Colossians 1:27). Today, we have many branches of the vine that want to keep the body in a "sin-conscious" instead of Christ anointing.

Verse 3: *"And I saw one of his heads as it were wounded to death; and his deadly wound was healed: and all the world wondered after the beast"*

Remember, we are not discussing a literal creature with seven heads. The "seven" is declaring the perfection and righteousness we have already obtained through Christ Jesus. When we do not live our lives according to who we are now, but with a "someday" when I get to heaven mentality, we nullify the power within us as sons of God and regress to the limitations of our carnal understanding. The church has given false power to the number six (the number of man or the old Adam) that only exists because of what religion has created to justify their doctrines. Jesus Christ did not throw a lifeline to the old Adam, but he went to the cross and identified himself AS the first Adam. The man that went into the tomb was not the man that came out of the tomb. The risen Savior was not recognized immediately as Jesus Christ. The same goes for us as His body. We have already been crucified in His crucifixion. Today we are new creations in Christ.

The deadly wound is the imagination of man that is contrary to the mind of Christ. Isaiah prophesied that in one day (Calvary), *"the LORD will cut off from Israel both head and tail, both palm branch and reed in a single day; the elders and prominent men are the head, the prophets who teach lies are the tail. Those who guide this people mislead them, and those who are guided are led astray"* (Isaiah 9:14-16, NIV).

Our salvation is found in Jesus Christ. That is the rock foundation of our faith that Jesus Christ is the only begotten Son of God. Our salvation is not about being a tag along with Jesus, but being dead with Him, and today we are alive in Christ as a new creation. All things of yesterday are gone. As we renew our mind by faith in this revelation, we manifest to our heart and body the truth of resurrection life according to the WORD, and not according to the world.

> *"So from now on we regard no one from a worldly point of view. Though we once regarded Christ in this way, we do so no longer. Therefore, if anyone is in Christ, the new creation has come: The old has gone, the new is here! All this is from God, who reconciled us to himself through*

Christ and gave us the ministry of reconciliation: that God was reconciling the world to himself in Christ, not counting people's sins against them. And he has committed to us the message of reconciliation. We are therefore Christ's ambassadors, as though God were making his appeal through us. We implore you on Christ's behalf: Be reconciled to God. God made him who had no sin to be sin for us, so that in him we might become the righteousness of God" (2 Corinthians 5:16-21).

When we do not appropriate our full Christ identity, the only thing we can offer others is the same limitations the world knows. Because the world will challenge believers to "prove" that their belief in Christianity is better than any other religion, a religious warfare takes place in the mind and hearts of believers thinking they have to prove God.

Think about this: If we are in Christ, and Christ is in us, and Christ is God; then who does that make us? What more is there for Jesus Christ to come back and do? Our time in this earthen vessel called flesh is for the purpose of growing up in Him to be the manifestation of Christ in and for the world. God said that HE is "I AM." Since we are the body of God; that makes us "I am" on a cellular level. Apart from God, we can do nothing, but in Christ, all things are possible.

How often do we add words to this completed statement (I am) when someone asks "How are you?" Do we respond with answers that agree with the WORD; the mind of Christ? Many times we ADD to the finished work of our identity by saying things like, "I am...sick; I am...poor; I am...depressed; I am...ugly; I am...lonely; I am...a sinner."

"Jesus looked at them and said, "With man this is impossible, but not with God; all things are possible with God." (Mark 10:27).

We do not need to beat ourselves up when this happens, but allow the Holy Spirit to speak the truth in love to our spirit saying,

"That may be what your old man use to say to you, but the truth of the Father who created you is this: you are healed, you are rich, you are happy full of joy, you are beautiful, you are surrounded by love, you are a royal priest in my kingdom now."

This is when God's grace really shines and transforms our knowledge of Him as God Almighty making of all into a personal relationship of knowing Him as Father. Otherwise, God would not have a family, and the earth would not be full of His glory; the sons of God. According to Rev. 22:18-19, *"For I testify unto every man that heareth the words of the prophecy of this book/Torah, If any man shall ADD unto these things, God shall add unto him the plagues that are written in this book/Torah: And if any man shall take away from the words of the book of this prophecy, God shall take away his part out of the book of life, and out of the holy city, and from the things which are written in this book."*

Verse 4: *"And they worshipped the dragon which gave power unto the beast: and they worshipped the beast, saying, who is like unto the beast? who is able to make war with him?"*

The "they" are Christians that have not understood they are already in Christ. Instead, their focus is on being a "sinner saved by grace" trying to get the "demons" out of their life and everyone else's around them. The church is represented as a "woman" who has the Spirit of God, but one who has been a harlot because she has been receiving "seed" from man's thinking processes (Matt. 16:23). In the world we start as a virgin, but in the WORD we start as a harlot and end up as a virgin (2 Corinthians 11:2).

Again, the dragon – amplified thought using the word of God for self - is the imagination that is controlling or "giving power" to the "beast" also known as the carnal man or Adamic nature (ego). He subtly uses logic and reasoning with the Scriptures to justify and ignite the senses of people. How often do we lift up certain preachers or speakers because they have charisma in their presentations; yet their whole message is about "someday when you get to heaven." There are no signs and wonders or resurrection of the dead. Instead, they preach through guilt, fear, and condemnation emphasizing a "hell" and "death" that Jesus has already destroyed.

Who can make war with this beast or the imagination of humanity who is using the power and authority of Scripture for their own glory? It is the power of the tongue that produces life and death. It is the imagination within us that will limit the fullness of who we are. Recalling what we studied in Rev. 12:10, *"And I heard a loud voice saying in heaven, now is come salvation, and strength, and the kingdom of our God, and the power of his Christ: for the accuser of our brethren is cast down, which accused them before our God day and night."*

The word "salvation" is the inclusive, sum of all the blessings bestowed by God on men in Christ through the Holy Spirit. When we understand that we have already received what we "think" we are going to receive "someday when we get to heaven" we can begin to

Repentance is not meant to beat us up with the wrath of God, but the pulling of the Father's love on our hearts for us to turn around and see the truth that will set up free.

function and operate as sons of God with the Father's power and authority on this earth. The sum of all the blessings is found in Jesus Christ who is the living WORD/Torah made flesh. He is the full potential of God's love and grace that can be released in His body through His many members around the world.

We have no power of our own to control the imagination of man that has power likened to a dragon. If you try to tell yourself "no, no, no" of your own strength you will find yourself wrestling with your imagination. However, because of the finished work Jesus Christ did for us at Calvary, God has given each of us the power to defeat this beast within ourselves when we boldly come to the mercy seat of God and allow our hearts and minds to be seated with Him surrounded by His love and grace. In this position, we have His authority to overcome the imagination of carnal man. God gives us His love and in turn we are able to love ourselves as He loves us. We are then able to extend unconditional love to others instead of judgments that are created by our carnal understanding (Luke 10:27). This is what Jacob encountered when he wrestled with his true identity in Genesis chapter 32.

God does not see any man's sin because He only sees us through Jesus Christ. Our frustrations we see in others often times are our own insecurities desiring others to change faster than what we see. When we pray with a heart of thanksgiving giving our concerns we see in the natural to the Father, He will send us His understanding through the Holy Spirit. We will know we are being led by the Spirit because of the fruit: Love, joy, peace, patience longsuffering, goodness, kindness, gentleness, and self-control.

Verse 5: *"And there was given unto him a mouth speaking great things and blasphemies; and power was given unto him to continue forty and two months."*

Please stay focused on who we are talking about in this verse. This is not a weird looking monster that we might see in movies or on television, nor is this a non-believer who strongly opposes God. This beast is the "old man" within us that has refused to die. Paul said, *"For if I build again those things which I destroyed, I make myself a transgressor. For I through the law of sin and death died to the law of sin and death that I might live to God"* (Galatians 2:18-19 NKJV).

"For we know that our old self was crucified with him so that the body of sin might be done away with, that we should no longer be slaves to sin because anyone who has died has been freed from sin. Now if we died with Christ,

we believe that we will also live with him. For we know that since Christ was raised from the dead, he cannot die again; death no longer has mastery over him. The death he died, he died to sin ONCE FOR ALL; but the life he lives, he lives to God. In the same way, count yourselves dead to sin but alive to God in Christ Jesus. Therefore do not let sin reign in your mortal body so that you obey its evil desires" (Romans 6:5-12, NIV).

How often do we hear spirit-filled believers in Christ use their tongue to judge and condemn others? How often do we hear those that are functioning in the five-fold ministry use the word of God to cause fear and anxiety in the body of Christ instead of the love of the Father? Notice this "beast" seems to speak great things or truths by using Scripture, but he also speaks things that do not line up with the nature and character of God. A simple reminder of this is when you hear Christians refer to themselves as "sinners saved by grace." God does not share his temple with anyone. We may still be in a growing stage of understanding which causes us to do things wrong, but we are not sinners! Even the children of God in the Old Testament never considered themselves separated from being God's family, yet Christians today think it sounds humble to call themselves a Christian and a sinner at the same time. This mindset is double-minded, lukewarm and has no place in the Holy of Holies where God's power and authority is to be released. Today, we have the mind of Christ! It is not to be mixed with our imagination.

The forty-two months symbolizes a time of ministry. It is not a literal three and a half years. Our lives are a time of ministry for us to grow in Christ (in love) so that we become equipped to function on this earth to do the Father's business as Jesus did. He demonstrated the Father's unconditional love for humanity by removing death, hell, and grave from us so we can know Him in our true identity as His sons. For some we recognize the calling on our life into ministry directly functioning in the church, and walk in it all our days in the flesh. For others, ministry may be outside of the literal church organization. Ministry may be on God's mountain of politics, economics, family, education, technology/communications, sciences, arts, etc. All of these are a part of the Father's networking the body of Christ together in unity, diversity, and love with Christ Jesus as the head.

Verse 6: *"And he opened his mouth in blasphemy against God, to blaspheme his name, and his tabernacle, and them that dwell in heaven."*

So who is this "he" opening his mouth and speaking against God? It is the believer in Christ that does not consider himself good enough to be considered a son of God. The tabernacle of God is the Holy of Holies or where He dwells within us. *"those things which proceed out of the mouth come forth from the heart; and they defile the man. For out of the heart proceed evil thoughts, murders, adulteries, fornications, thefts, false witness, blasphemies:"* (Matt. 15:18-19). Our hearts should be declaring "Holy, Holy, Holy is the Lord God Almighty maker of Heaven and Earth that by Him, through Him, and for Him are all things created; for He is all in all."

When Isaiah saw the Lord high and exacted, and heard the holy angels singing Holy, Holy, Holy…Isaiah said,

"Woe to me!" I cried. "I am ruined! For I am a man of unclean lips, and I live among a people of unclean lips, and my eyes have seen the King, the Lord *Almighty." Then one of the seraphim flew to me with a live coal in his hand, which he had taken with tongs from the altar. With it he touched my mouth and said, "See, this has touched your lips; your guilt is taken away and your sin atoned for." Then I heard the voice of the Lord saying, "Whom shall I send? And who will go for us?" And I said, "Here am I. Send me!" (Isaiah 6:5-8).*

The Father desires to hear His WORD spoken through our mouth, not a beaten up believer that is stuck in negativity.

The war that goes on around us is created within us. We create our own atmosphere by the thoughts released through our mouths. In John 10:34, Jesus quotes, "Ye are gods..." to the Jews, which had already been written in Psalm 82:6-8, *"I have said, Ye are gods; and all of you are children of the Most High. But ye shall die like men, and fall like one of the princes. Arise, O God, judge the earth: for thou shalt inherit all nations."* Notice, Jesus only quoted the first three words to them. Since they knew the Scriptures, Jesus only had to give reference to the Psalm in order for their minds to finish the rest of the verses. It should have been a word of encouragement for them to know they were already children of the Most High God, but because the prophecy included "the bondage of dying as men and falling as princes," they instead took offense and accused Jesus of declaring blasphemy.

Notice also that the word "gods" in verse 6 of Psalm 82 is the same word used for "God" in verse 8. It is the word Elohim (el-o-heem'); plural of gods in the ordinary sense; but specifically used (in the plural thus, especially with the article) of the supreme God. If we considered ourselves "gods" alone we would be declaring blasphemy; but as children of the "Most High God" ('elyown (el-yone'); an elevation - the Supreme, we then are ruling and reigning in power and position that flows through us coming from our Heavenly Father. This is only accomplished when we know who we are in Christ through the life, death, and resurrection of Jesus Christ.

There is subtlety to what is taking place in verse 6. This is not a world leader shouting blasphemy against God. These are people that have been "born again" by the Spirit of God, yet they have not yet come out of the bondage of the "Adam" identity. They harbor ideas and thoughts such as: "I am a sinner that has been saved by grace; even though I am a Christian, I will never be perfect until I get to heaven; I came from Adam and am just a poor wretched human being not worthy of anything." This is BLASPHEMY coming out of the mouth of God's children, yet Christians are continuously expressing these thoughts in the house of God. In the natural, this would be like cussing, and parents would be washing their children's' mouths out with soap.

"Through faith we understand that the worlds were framed by the word of God, so that things which are seen were not made of things which do appear" (Hebrews 11:3). Isaiah 29:16 declares, *"You turn things upside down, as if the potter were thought to be like the clay! Shall what is formed say to him who formed it, 'He did not make me' or Can the pot say of the potter, 'He knows nothing'?"* (NIV).

"God said to Moses, "I AM WHO I AM. This is what you are to say to the Israelites: 'I AM has sent me to you.'" (Exodus 3:14). The Father is coming after His identity in us to unveil that we are the "I am" in the I AM.

Verse 7: *"And it was given unto him to make war with the saints, and to overcome them: and power was given him over all kindred, and tongues, and nations."*

The word "with" should be the word "met-ah" meaning "in the midst of." The war that is going on in this verse is not a war between men, but the war between what God says in our heart and mind versus what our imagination tries to create and justify with Scripture. Our natural man wants to exalt itself above God instead of being in God; not by considering ourselves "holier than God," but by denying the fullness of who we are in Christ. *"But if, while we seek to be justified by Christ, we ourselves also are found sinners, is therefore Christ the minister of sin? God forbid. For if I build again the things which I destroyed, I make myself a transgressor. For I through the law am dead to the law, that I might live unto God. I am crucified with Christ: nevertheless I live; yet not I, but Christ liveth in me: and the life which I now live in the flesh I live by the faith of the Son of God, who loved me, and gave himself for me. I do not frustrate the grace of God"* (Galatians 2:17-21).

While our thoughts are still as children of God, the imagination has power over our humanity (kindred, nations, and tongues). This is all part of the growth process. God is in total control of what is happening and as our humanity battles with the seed of God in us we will grow up in Christ. It may not happen according to our timing, but it will happen. It's just like the different stages we experience in natural growth and development. Many times our bodies will say we are at one age, but our minds will war by demanding that we are another age. This is why we see 12-year olds trying to be 20, or 40-year olds trying to look 25.

In the spirit realm, we have been crucified and resurrected with Him, but our humanity will try to argue with the mind of Christ in us saying that we still have to die and that we cannot come into the fullness of our inheritance until someday when we get to heaven. God is Spirit and Heaven is where He abodes. Paul tells us in Ephesians 1:10-12, *"That in the dispensation of the fullness of times he might gather together in one all things in Christ, both which are in heaven, and which are on earth; even in him: In whom also we have obtained an inheritance, being predestinated according to the purpose of him who worketh all things after the counsel of his own will: That we should be to the praise of his glory, who first trusted in Christ."*

It is good news that the imagination cannot win a war that has already been won through the death and resurrection of Jesus Christ. He died once and for all over 2000 years ago. His death is my death, and His resurrection is my resurrection! The negatives of our lives are just part of the process to bring out the positive within our spirits for the purpose of teaching us to *"count it all joy when ye fall into divers temptations; Knowing this, that the trying of your faith worketh patience"* (James 1:2-3).

Verse 8: *"And all that dwell upon the earth shall worship him, whose names are not written in the book of life of the Lamb slain from the foundation of the world."*

If we were to read this verse with our natural understanding, the way the church has preached it for hundreds of years; it would bring separation and division to the body of Christ. The church has taught that those whose names are written in the book of Life are going to heaven and those who are not included because they never prayed a "sinner's prayer" are going to hell. Again, God is Spirit, and it is *only by the Holy Spirit releasing the wisdom of God through the mind of Christ in us that the revelation of Jesus Christ can be manifested out of us.* The "earth" is not the literal planet, but those that insist upon camping around the outer court (dust company), or middle court (sand company) in their Christian life.

The book of Life is not a big clerical book that angels are writing or erasing names in. It is the people of God living their life by the faith of Jesus Christ who gave His live for us before the foundation of the world. There is no death in Him. The book is the Torah that was with God in the beginning. Paul said in 2 Cor. 3:1-3, *"Do we begin again to commend ourselves? or need we, as some others, epistles of commendation to you, or letters of commendation from you? Ye are our epistle written in our hearts, known and read of all men: Forasmuch as ye are manifestly declared to be the epistle of Christ ministered by us, written not with ink, but with the Spirit of the living God; not in tables of stone, but in fleshy tables of the heart."*

"In the beginning God created the heavens and the earth" (Genesis 1:1). The word God is Elohim, the creator of all. Notice heavens is plural and earth is one. Jesus Christ is the first fruit of many brethren/heavens that were with Him before the foundation of the earth.

"In the beginning was the Word/Torah, and the Word/Torah was with God, and the Word/Torah was God. He/Torah was with God in the beginning. Through him/Torah all things were made; without him/Torah nothing was made that has been made. In him/Torah was life, and that life/Torah was the light/seed of God in ALL mankind. The light/God shines in the darkness/ignorance, and the darkness/ignorance has not overcome the

LIGHT" (John 1:1-5). *"The Word/Torah became flesh/Jesus Christ and made his dwelling among us. We have seen his glory, the glory of the one and only Son, who came from the Father, full of grace* (the dunamis power of the Holy Spirit) *and truth* (the fullness of LIFE, LIGHT, LOVE, ETERNALLY NOW). (John 1:14). Jesus Christ is the incarnate Torah, the glory of God that was with Him in the beginning. Today, as Christ one's we are the living epistles of the WORD made flesh, the Torah that is not written with ink, but with the Spirit of the living God on our heart (Hebrews 8:8-10).

If we believe that He died and has been resurrected, then there must also be a firstfruit company of people called the church that believe they are not supposed to go through a natural death since they have already died with Him. This is the gospel the disciples preached and shared with the many nations that stirred up controversy and brought forth persecution. Paul emphasized this in Galatians 2:20, *"I am crucified with Christ: nevertheless I live; yet not I, but Christ liveth in me: and the life which I now live in the flesh I live by the faith of the Son of God, who loved me, and gave himself for me."*

Jesus is the head of Christ, and the church is the body. There cannot be a resurrected head and a dying body. The body must have the same LIFE flowing through it that the head has; resurrected life. When Paul explained who the "unknown God" was to the Athenians on Mars Hill (the one they worshipped as the God of heaven and earth) he emphasized that the main difference between the unknown God (Jesus Christ) and the other gods was the power He had in resurrecting the dead (Acts 17).

> *"God, who made the world and everything in it, since He is Lord of heaven and earth, does not dwell in temples made with hands. Nor is He worshiped with men's hands, as though He needed anything, since He gives to ALL life, breath, and ALL things. And He has made from ONE blood EVERY nation of men to dwell on ALL the*

face of the earth, and has determined their preappointed times and the boundaries of their dwellings, so that they should seek the Lord, in the hope that they might grope for Him and find Him, though He is not far from each one of us; for IN HIM we live and move and have our being, as also some of your own poets have said, 'For we are also His offspring.' Therefore, since we are the offspring of God, we ought not to think that the Divine Nature is like gold or silver or stone, something shaped by art and man's devising. Truly, these times of ignorance God overlooked, BUT NOW commands ALL men everywhere to repent, because HE has appointed a day on which He will judge the world in righteousness by THE MAN whom HE has ordained. He has given assurance of this to ALL by raising Him from the dead. And when they heard of THE RESURRECTION OF THE DEAD, some mocked, while others said, "We will hear you again on this matter." So Paul departed from among them. However, some men joined him and believed, among them Dionysius the Areopagite, a woman named Damaris, and others with them" (Acts 17:24-34, NKJV).

The word "foundation" is the Greek word "kat-ab-ol-ay" meaning "conception." The word "world" is the word "kos'-mos" meaning "the orderly arrangement of creation." In the beginning, before Genesis 1:1, God had created a way for all of His creation to return to Him so that the Scripture had already been fulfilled declaring that God is all in all (1 Corinthians 15:28). Jesus Christ was slain BEFORE the foundation of the world; before the fall of Adam. He died for the sins of the world before there was a world *"who has blessed us in the heavenly realms with every spiritual blessing in Christ. For he chose us in him before the creation of the world to be holy and blameless in his sight"* (Ephesians 1:3-4, NIV).

Verse 9: *"If any man has an ear, let him hear."*

In the original text the words "if any man" are not written. The verse should read "have an ear, let him hear." This is a time to pause and consider what the Holy Spirit is saying to each of us. He has not been talking about a someday occurrence of destruction, but the process of what is taking place in each person (past, present, and future) as a corporate body for the manifestation of Jesus Christ on this earth. *"You answer us with awesome deeds of righteousness, O God our Savior, the hope of all the ends of the earth"* (Psalm 65:5, NIV); *"Remember to extol his work, which men have praised in song. All humankind has seen it; men gaze on it from afar. How great is God-beyond our understanding"* (Job 36:24-26, NIV).

Remember, the Bible that Jesus, John, Paul, Peter, Jude, and James used to write their letters in the New Testament was the Tanakh, or the Old Testament. Their life manuscript or constitution was the Torah, or the first five books of Moses.

Verse 10: *"He that leadeth into captivity shall go into captivity: he that killeth with the sword must be killed with the sword. Here is the patience and the faith of the saints."*

John is telling us in this verse the same thing that we read in Matthew 7:1-2, *"Do not judge, or you too will be judged. For in the same way you judge others, you will be judged, and with the measure you use, it will be measured to you"* (NIV). The "sword" is the WORD/Torah of God. How often have we heard Scripture quoted to justify a "yea or nea" situation that pertains to someone else? As new creatures in Christ (2 Corinthians 5:17) there cannot be any condemnation (Romans 8:1).

"Here is the patience and the faith of the saints." This is one of those places that holds a mystery to be searched out by those that hunger and thirst for God. First of all, if we have been crucified with Him and the life we NOW live is by the faith of the Son of God (Gal. 2:20), everything we need in the flesh has already been provided. Jesus Christ never once asked the Father for anything for Himself, but always for others.

This should be our lives today, to give unconditionally to others despite the warfare of our natural reasoning and understanding about the situation. If we are going through something, let our prayer be for the Father to show us who He is at this season that He could not be before, so that we can go through the issue as an overcomer to be a blessing to someone else.

Let's read James 1:2-8, *"Consider it pure joy, my brothers, whenever you face trials of many kinds, because you know that the testing of your faith develops perseverance. Perseverance must finish its work so that you may be mature and complete, not lacking anything. If any of you lacks wisdom, he should ask God, who gives generously to all without finding fault, and it will be given to him. But when he asks, he must believe and not doubt, because he who doubts is like a wave of the sea, blown and tossed by the wind. That man should not think he will receive anything from the Lord; he is a double-minded man, unstable in all he does"* (NIV).

A key to understanding these verses is to read it the way it was written instead of the way it has been translated. Go to *"If any of you lacks wisdom"* and read from there first, then go back to verse 2. It takes the wisdom of God to be able to count it all joy in the midst of trials and persecution.

Paul writes in Romans 15:1-7, *"We who are strong ought to bear with the failings of the weak and not to please ourselves. Each of us should please his neighbor for his good, to build him up. For even Christ did not please himself but, as it is written: "The insults of those who insult you have fallen on me." For everything that was written in the past was written to teach us, so that through endurance and the encouragement of the Scriptures we might have hope. May the God who gives endurance and encouragement give you a spirit of unity among yourselves as you follow Christ Jesus, so that with one heart and mouth you may glorify the God and Father of our Lord Jesus Christ. Accept one another, then, just as Christ accepted you, in order to bring praise to God"* (NIV).

Verse 11: *"And I beheld another beast coming up out of the earth; and he had two horns like a lamb, and he spake as a dragon."*

Notice that this beast is coming from the earth or the worldly mentality of man. The two horns represent what is going on in the head of this person. The "lamb" signifies that this is a believer in Jesus Christ, who "speaks like a dragon" (one whose heart is full of religious mixture.) Jesus refers to this type of believer as a viper when he says in Matthew 12:34-37, *"You brood of vipers, how can you who are evil say anything good? For out of the overflow of the heart the mouth speaks. The good man brings good things out of the good stored up in him, and the evil man brings evil things out of the evil stored up in him. But I tell you that men will have to give account on the day of judgment for every careless word they have spoken. For by your words you will be acquitted, and by your words you will be condemned"* (NIV).

Verse 12: *"And he exerciseth all the power of the first beast before him, and causeth the earth and them which dwell therein to worship the first beast, whose deadly wound was healed."*

We have discussed the first beast and the deadly wound that was healed in verse 3. What is this deadly wound? It is the antichrist, or self focused spirit, that does war in our heads with our true identity as children of God. This verse is describing the religious system called the church that is functioning in their own intellectual power and strength to justify their carnally minded interpretations of Scripture. Because of ignorance to the ways of God, the "first beast" has given power to church doctrines, academic education, theocracy, and church finances to stir up the imagination, or "deadly wound," versus giving God all glory and praise with a goal to unite the body of Christ as one.

As believers in Christ, it is pertinent for us to always have teachable spirits that are receptive to the ways of God. When we give more strength and power to the doctrines and beliefs of the church than the possibility that we might be missing the truth of God, then we are worshipping that first beast (SELF). We must look at every word and every accusation that comes to us and learn from it with a heart's desire to change anything that needs to be changed giving thanks to God for opening our ears to hear what the Holy Spirit revealed.

Verse 13: *"And he doeth great wonders, so that he maketh fire come down from heaven on the earth in the sight of men."*

This "second beast" is not a separate person from the "first beast," but are those in the position of ministering and teaching others. These may be people that have been lifted to a position in the church to have power and authority (i.e. pastors, teachers, evangelists, prophets, apostles, leaders, Sunday school teachers, elders, deacons, church administrators, counselors, etc.) that know the Scriptures and the power of God. They use it to bring justification and control by demonstrating "great wonders" which plays upon the senses and emotions of those they were given by God to be receiving His wisdom and understanding.

The "first beast" pollutes the outer court with justification mixed with the grace of God. The "second beast" adds this mixture of grace and self-justification with the imagination of self-gratification to pollute the middle court. This prevents those in the middle court from manifesting the love and life of Jesus Christ. Their prophesies come through what is happening in the world instead of by the Spirit of God. Since there is power in the words that are spoken, "great wonders" will be manifested. These leaders will try to give glory to God, but the problem is that their declarations do not line up with the character and nature of our Heavenly Father. They are using Scripture to justify their own imagination of what is going on in the world.

> *"We are all children of God, but no one is all God. It takes all of humankind to form the body of Christ."*

What takes place from this are wars and rumors of wars that have been created by men who justify and separate themselves from others using the name of God. We are all children of God, but no one is all God. It takes all of humankind to form the body of Christ. That body can only function properly with the mind of Jesus Christ who is the head. The responsibility we each carry is to BE who we were created to BE, manifesting Christ, not our own thoughts and ideas. A dead man is dead. The life we are to be living NOW is in Christ. In Matthew 7:3-5, Jesus told the religious leaders (second beast), *"why do you look at the speck in your brother's eye, but do not consider the plank in your own eye? Or how can you say to your brother, 'Let me remove the speck from your eye'; and look, a plank is in your own eye? Hypocrite! First remove the plank from your own eye, and then you will see clearly to remove the speck out of your brother's eye"* (NKJV).

Many church leaders are working for a paycheck and have not truly been called by God. If their salaries and perks were taken away it would be interesting to see how many would voluntarily serve in ministry. Many of these people are performing theatrics on a platform, emphasizing the need to give for the needy or for the building fund, while they go home to their mansions, Mercedes, and house cleaners. Many times they play on people's emotions by showing pictures of children that are starving, yet they give very little themselves.

True leaders serve from the position of "walking in another's shoes." Pastors do not have to experience every problem or challenge in life to be a good pastor, but they must realize that they are in a position to bless and unite (purify with fire) the body of Christ. They do not judge by the outward appearance of a negative situation, but find the root of understanding the heart of what God is working out in people's lives.

God sees His finished work and purpose in us of His creation. He established in the heavens before we were conceived in our mother's womb. Just as we can pick up an acorn which carries everything necessary for a beautiful oak tree, so also the totality of our identity in Christ, created in the image of God, is already in us. We battle with the beast of our ego and the negativity from others that only speak of our outward man. God speaks to our heart.

Verse 14: *"And deceives them that dwell on the earth by the means of those miracles which he had power to do in the sight of the beast; saying to them that dwell on the earth, that they should make an image to the beast, which had the wound by a sword, and did live."*

Who is doing the deceiving and who is being deceived? In Malachi Chapters 1 and 2, the Lord refers to the deceivers as the priests who had brought "strange fire" to the alter. They went through the motions of ritual cleansing for themselves and the people, but their hearts were not giving glory and honor to God. Aaron's sons saw what their father did when coming to the Holy Place and presenting himself before God, but they didn't understand the why behind what was happening. God will share His glory with no other spirits. He communes with the Holy Spirit in us. Without faith it is impossible to please God.

In Matthew 27:63, it was the chief priests and Pharisees who referred to Jesus Christ as being the deceiver. Then in 2 John 7-9 we read, *"For many deceivers* (those preaching the word of God) *have gone out into the world who do not confess Jesus Christ as coming in the flesh* (resurrection of the body of Christ). *This is a deceiver and an antichrist. Look to yourselves, that we do not lose those things we worked for, but that we may receive a full reward. Whoever transgresses and does not abide in the doctrine of Christ* (unconditional love to all with the power of resurrection life) *does not have God* (eternal life, love, light). *He who abides in the doctrine of Christ has both* (as He is, so are we in this world) *the Father and the Son"* (NKJV).

Those that are being deceived are not the non-believers, but Christians who abide in the word from the perspective of receiving their inheritance "someday" when they get "somewhere" called heaven. They are people that hang on to their past and have been taught that they will never be good enough for God because of the sin of Adam. Deception comes when we do not live by faith, but by signs and wonders.

Verse 15: *"And he had power to give life unto the image of the beast, that the image of the beast should both speak, and cause that as many as would not worship the image of the beast should be killed."*

A key word in this verse is "image." Where are images created? They are in our thought processes. The "image" of the beast tries to emphasize a killing of the old Adam. The "beast" will try to use Scripture to justify guilt and

> *"Jesus did not experience miracles, but He was the miracle manifested to others."*

condemnation. Jesus Christ is the faithful witness who declares we are in Him where there is no condemnation (Romans 8:1). If we know we are new creations in Christ, we don't need to be killed again. We already died with Him at Calvary, and today we live a resurrected life in Christ by His faith in us. Jesus did not experience miracles, but He was the miracle manifested to others.

Verse 16: *"And he causeth all, both small and great, rich and poor, free and bond, to receive a mark in their right hand, or in their foreheads."*

I have addressed this "mark of the beast" issue earlier of what John was talking about; but to make sure we do not have any preconceived ideas, the "mark of the beast" was the first Adam; the number of man. Because we were born in this flesh, we received the mind of humanity (forehead mark), which creates the thought (mark of the right hand). However, our flesh is not who we are, but the vessel we are living in. While living in our natural bodies, God is teaching us about our Christ nature even when the old Adam nature tries to separate us from Him (Gen. 6:5). In this process of growth He is our Father who will never leave us or forsake us no matter how much we may stumble (Deut. 31:6). He is training us up in the way we should go (Proverbs 22:6).

The right hand signifies authority of the one holding the scepter. This was given to the tribe of Judah to lead with praise and worship unto God in battle. Jesus came into the world through this tribe to signify He is the King of kings, the other tribes, and Lord of lords, the other land owners of the whole house of Israel. Ephraim's tribe was given the birthright. When the birthright, the true church today, and the blessing come together, the Jewish nation as one, we will have the prophesy fulfillment of Ezekiel 37:23-28,

> *"They will be my people, and I will be their God. "My servant David will be king over them, and they will all have one shepherd. They will follow my laws and be careful to keep my decrees. They will live in the land I gave to my servant Jacob, the land where your ancestors lived. They and their children and their children's children will live there forever, and David my servant will be their prince forever. I will make a covenant of peace with them; it will be an everlasting covenant. I will establish them and increase their numbers, and I will put my sanctuary among them forever. My dwelling place will be with them; I will be their God, and they will be my people. Then the nations will know that I the LORD make Israel holy, when my sanctuary is among them forever.'"*

This is the sign that is written in the Old Testament of the Lord's return for a bride company made of the whole house of Israel ruling and reigning with Him in heavenly places as the Kingdom of God in the earth. Today we are in the rehearsal phase of a bride preparing herself on how to be not only the bride, but the wife and co-heir of the throne of God.

Verse 17: *"And that no man might buy or sell, save he that had the mark, or the name of the beast, or the number of his name."*

This verse has nothing to do with being able to buy food or sell merchandise. It has nothing to do with being tattooed with the number "666," UPC Codes, or computer chips being implanted in the skin. As long as we continue to lift up the "mark of the beast" or the old Adam, we will buy what the beast is selling. When we know that we are new creations in Christ and that we are the righteousness of Christ today, then there will be no old Adam, and we won't be buying what the "beast" is selling.

Let us not frustrate the grace and mercy of God, but renew our minds to the knowledge of Christ as we are seated with Him on the mercy seat of God. Jesus Christ died once and for all. There doesn't need to be another killing, but a renewing of who we are today in Christ because His death was our death and His resurrection is the life we now live.

Verse 18: *"Here is wisdom. Let him that hath understanding count the number of the beast: for it is the number of a man; and his number is Six hundred threescore and six."*

This is not a literal number, but a triple witness of humanity. We are a triple being in oneness (spirit, soul, and body) and by His Spirit God is working through our humanity to perfect our thinking in order to bring us back to our true identity in

> *"Hear, O Israel: The LORD our God, the LORD is one" (Deuteronomy 6:4).*

Christ. God is not separating us, but bringing us together in His love that surpasses all understanding. It is the Feast of Tabernacles, the Feast of Ingathering, and the Feast of Oneness. Christ is all and in all (Col. 3:11).

To get rid of the "mark of the beast" or humankind, we must renew our mind (Rom. 12:2) with the "mark of the cross."

"Knowing this, that our old man is (already has been) *crucified with him, that the body of sin might be* (has been) *destroyed, that henceforth we should not serve sin* (our imagination). *For he that is dead is freed from sin* (carnal understanding). *NOW if we be* (already) *dead with Christ, we believe that we shall also live* (now) *with him: Knowing that Christ being* (has been) *raised from the dead dieth no more; death hath no more dominion over him. For in that he died, he died unto sin once: but in that he liveth, he liveth unto God. LIKEWISE reckon ye also yourselves to be dead indeed unto sin, but alive unto God through Jesus Christ our Lord"* (Romans 6:6-11).

"For Christ did not send me to baptize, but to preach the gospel–not with words of human wisdom, lest the cross of Christ be emptied of its power. For the message of the cross is foolishness to those who are perishing, but to us who are being saved it is the power of God. For it is written: "I will destroy the wisdom of the wise; the intelligence of the intelligent I will frustrate." Where is the wise man? Where is the scholar? Where is the philosopher of this age? Has not God made foolish the wisdom of the world? For since in the wisdom of God the world through its wisdom did not know him, God was pleased through the foolishness of what was preached to save those who believe. Jews demand miraculous signs and Greeks look for wisdom, but we preach Christ crucified: a stumbling block to Jews and foolishness to Gentiles, but to those whom God has called, both Jews and Greeks, Christ the power of God and the wisdom of God. For the foolishness of God is wiser than man's wisdom, and the weakness of God is stronger than man's strength" (1 Corinthians 1:17-25, NIV).

Notes of Reflection

What were your immediate thoughts in this chapter?

_____

_____

_____

_____

_____

What preconceived thoughts did you have before reading this chapter?

_____

_____

_____

_____

_____

What new information did you learn?

_____

_____

_____

_____

_____

Does this information seem confusing or liberating? Why?

_____

_____

_____

_____

_____

Scripture References

The following are Scriptures that will be an encouragement for you to step out of your comfort zone of traditional teachings on Christianity. As I began my research, the word "ALL" began to stand out bringing me to ask the Father, if "all" really meant "ALL." The Holy Spirit challenged me with the question, "How big is your faith to want to believe that "all" really means "ALL"? The extent of your faith is what will determine "ALL" in your life. It was then that the Lord reminded me that, *I could do ALL things through Christ which strengthened me*" (Philippians 4:13)

These Scriptures have been taken from the King James Version of the Bible. The parenthesis are mine, along with capitalizing the word "ALL" to help you reconsider the way you may have been interpreting our Father's love letters in the past.

"Which was the son of Enos, which was the son of Seth, which was the son of Adam, which was the Son of God." (Luke 3:38)

"In the day that God created man, in the likeness (image) *of God* (himself) *made he him: Male and female* (both Adam) *created he them; and blessed them, and called their name Adam, in the day when they were created."* (Genesis 5:1-2)

"And in thee shall ALL families of the earth be blessed." (Genesis 12:3)

"The Lord is gracious, and full of compassion; slow to anger, and of great mercy. The Lord is good to ALL: and his tender mercies are over ALL his works. ALL thy works shall praise thee, O Lord; and thy saints shall bless thee." (Psalm 145:8-10)

"For since by man came death, by man came also the resurrection of the dead. For as in Adam ALL die, even so in Christ shall ALL be made alive." (I Corinthians 15:21-22)

"For it is God which worketh in you both to will and to do of his good pleasure." (Philippians 2:13)

"Do ALL things without murmurings and disputing: That ye may be blameless and harmless, the sons of God, without rebuke, in the midst of a crooked and perverse nation, among whom ye shine as lights in the world." (Philippians 2:14-15)

"Let this mind be in you, which was also in Christ Jesus: Who, being in the form of God, thought it not robbery to be equal with God." (Philippians 2:5-6)

"For the Father judgeth no man, but hath committed all judgment unto the Son." (John 5:22)

"Verily, verily, I say unto you, the Son can do nothing of himself, but what he seeth the Father do: for what things so ever he doeth, these also doeth the Son likewise." (John 5:19)

"ALL things were made by him; and without him was not any thing made that was made. In him was life: and the life was the light of men." (John 1:3-4)

"But as many as received him to them gave he power to become the sons of God, even to them that believe on him name." (John 1:12)

"Jesus saith unto them, 'My meat is to do the will of him that sent me, and to finish his work.'" (John 4:34)

"The Lord is not slack concerning his promise, as some men count slackness; but is longsuffering to us-ward, not willing that any should perish, but that ALL should come to repentance." (2 Peter 3:9)

"Not by the works of righteousness which we have done, but according to his mercy he saved us, by the washing of regeneration, and renewing of the Holy Ghost; which he shed on us abundantly through Jesus Christ our Savior; that being justified by his grace, we should be made heirs according to the hope of eternal life." (Titus 3: 5-7)

"Therefore as by the offense of one judgment came upon ALL men to condemnation; even so by the righteousness of one the free gift came upon ALL men unto justification of life." (Romans 5:18)

"There is therefore now no condemnation to them which are in Christ Jesus who walk not after the flesh, but after the Spirit." (Romans 8:1)

"For I am persuaded, that neither death, nor life, nor angels, nor principalities, nor powers, nor things present, nor things to come, nor height, nor depth, nor any other creature, shall be able to separate us from the love of God, which is in Christ Jesus our Lord." (Romans 8:38-39)

"Know ye not that ye are the temple of God, and that the Spirit of God dwelleth in you?" (I Corinthians 3:16)

"Let no man glory in men, For ALL things are yours; whether Paul, or Apollos, or Cephas, or the world, or life, or death, or things present, or things to come; ALL are yours; And ye are Christ's, and Christ is God's." (I Corinthians 3:21-23)

"For by him were ALL things created, that are in heaven, and that are in earth, visible and invisible, whether they be thrones, or dominions, or

principalities, or powers: ALL things were created by him, and for him: and he is before ALL things, and by him ALL things consist." (Colossians 1:16-17)

"And hath made of one blood ALL nations of men for to dwell on all the face of the earth, and hath determined the times before appointed, and the abounds of their habitation; that they should seek the Lord, if haply they might feel after him, and find him, though he be not far from every one of us: for in him we live, and move, and have our being; as certain also of your own poets have said, For we are also his offspring." (Acts 17:26-28)

"Therefore if any man be in Christ, he is a new creature: old things are passed away; behold ALL things are become new. And ALL things are of God, who hath reconciled us to himself by Jesus Christ, and hath given to us the ministry of reconciliation."
(2 Corinthians 5:17-18)

"I am crucified with Christ: nevertheless I live; yet not I, but Christ liveth in me: and the life which I now live in the flesh I live by the faith of the Son of God, who loved me, and gave himself for me." (Galatians 2:20)

"And if ye be Christ's, then are ye Abraham's seed, and heirs according to the promise." (Galatians 3:29)

"And because ye are sons, God hath sent forth the Spirit of his Son into your hearts, crying Abba, Father." (Galatians 4:6)

"Verily, verily, I say unto you, if a man keeps my saying, he shall never see death." (John 8:51)

"Jesus answered them, 'Is not written in your law, I said ye are gods?'" (John 10:34)

"Now is the judgment of this world: now shall the prince of this world be cast out. And I if I be lifted up from the earth will draw ALL

men unto me. *This he said, signifying what death he should die."* (John 12:31-33)

"Therefore, leaving the principles of the doctrine of Christ, let us go on unto perfection; laying again the foundation of repentance from dead works, and of faith toward God, of the doctrine of baptisms, and of laying on of hands, and of resurrection of the dead, and of eternal judgment." (Hebrews 6:1-2)

"We know that we have passed from death unto life, because we love the brethren. He that loveth not his brother abideth in death." (1 John 3:14)

"Ye are of God, little children, and have overcome them: because greater is he that is in you, than he that is in the world." (1 John 4:4)

"Beloved, let us love one another: for love is of God; and every one that loveth is born of God, and knoweth God." (1 John 4:7)

"That which was from the beginning, which we have heard, which we have seen with our eyes, which we have looked upon, and our hands have handled, of the Word of life." (1 John 1:1)

"And these things write we unto you, that your joy may be full. This then is the message which we have heard of him, and declare unto you, that God is light, and in him is no darkness at ALL." (1 John 1:4-5)

"Then Jesus said unto them, 'Yet a little while is the light with you. Walk while ye have the light, lest darkness come upon you: for he that walketh in darkness knoweth not whither he goeth. While ye have light, believe in the light, that ye may be the children of light.'" (John 12:35-36)

"Ye have not chosen me, but I have chosen you, and ordained you, that ye should go and bring forth fruit, and that your fruit should remain: that whatsoever ye shall ask of the Father in my name, he may give it you." (John 15:16)

"Ye are the light of the world. A city that is set on a hill cannot be hid. Let your light so shine before men, that they may see your good works, and glorify your Father which is in heaven." (Matthew 5:14, 16)

"Blessed are the pure in heart: for they shall see God. Blessed are the peacemakers: for they shall be called the children of God." (Matthew 5:8-9)

"Be careful for nothing, but in every thing by prayer and supplication with thanksgiving let your requests by made known unto God. And the peace of God, which passeth all understanding, shall keep your hearts and minds through Christ Jesus. Finally, brethren, whatsoever things are true, whatsoever things are honest, whatsoever things are just, whatsoever things are pure, whatsoever things are lovely, whatsoever thing are of good report; if there be any virtue, and if there be any praise, think on these things." (Philippians 3:6-8)

"Rejoice in the Lord always; and again I say, Rejoice." (Philippians 3:4)

"As he is, so are we in this world." (1 John 4:17)

APPENDIX

Our Identity in Christ Today

TODAY, I AM the righteousness of God in Christ Jesus!
2 Corinthians 5:21

TODAY, I AM Blessed with ALL Spiritual blessings in heavenly places!
Ephesians 1:3

TODAY, I AM born again by the word of God!
1 Peter 23:1

TODAY, I AM redeemed by the blood!
Ephesians 1:7

TODAY, I AM complete in Jesus!
Colossians 2:9-10

TODAY, I AM not a sinner. ALL sin identity has been nailed to the cross!
Colossians 2:14

TODAY, I AM sealed with the HOLY SPIRIT!
Ephesians 1:13

TODAY, I rule and reign in the name of Jesus!
Romans 5:17

TODAY, I AM more than a conqueror! I take dominion!
Romans 8:37, Genesis 1:28

TODAY, I AM able to do ALL things through CHRIST who strengthens me!
Philippians 4:13

TODAY, I AM strengthened in ALL might by His glorious power!
Colossians 1: 9-10

TODAY, I AM able to command the powers of darkness in the name of Jesus!
Mark 16:17

TODAY, I AM triumphant in Jesus' name! His word never returns void! I come boldly before the throne of grace receiving unconditional mercy and love.
2 Corinthians 2:14, Isaiah 55:11, Hebrews 4:16

When I know the name of God, I become the duplicate of that name manifesting those attributes and apprehending that character which the name denotes. This signifies the active presence of His glory: And the WORD BECAME FLESH!

Reading Resources

Allen, J.H., *Judah's Sceptre and Joseph's Birthright*, (Destiny Publishers, Mass., 1917).

Arno, Richard and Phyllis, *Creation Therapy*, (Sarasota Academy of Christian Counseling, Florida, 2012).

Benner, Jeff A., *The Ancient Hebrew Language and Alphabet*, (Virtualbookworm Publishing, 2004).

Blosser, Don, Timothy J. Dailey, Randy Petersen, Dietrich Gruen, *Jesus His Life and Times*, (Publications International, Ltd, Illinois, 1999).

Connolly, Peter, *The Holy Land*, (Oxford University Press, Oxford, 1994).

Cooke, Graham, *Radical Perceptions*, (Brilliant BookHouse, California, 2011).

Daniels, Will, *Understanding the Oneness of God* (WestBow Press, Indiana 2014).

Drummonds, Bishop A., *Bringing Forth the Sons of God*, (Iuniverse, NE, 2004).

Drummonds, Bishop A., *God's Redemption for All*, (Iuniverse, NY, 2007).

Grunfeld, Dayan Dr., *The Sabbath*, (Feldheim Publishers, Jerusalem, 2014).

Huch, Larry, *The Torah Blessing*, (Whitaker House, PA, 2009).

Hurnard, Hannah, *Hinds' Feet on High Places Devotional*, (Destiny Image, PA., 2013).

Johnson, Bill, *When Heaven Invades Earth*, (Destiny Image, PA, 2003).

Johnston, Robert D., *Numbers in the Bible*, (Kregel Publications, Michigan, 1990).

Kenyon, E.W., *The Blood Covenant*, (Kenyon's Gospel Publishing Society, USA, 2012).

Mason, Phil, *Quantum Glory*, XPpublishing, Arizona, 2010).

Messer, Rabbi Ralph, *Torah: Law or Grace?* (Simchat Torah Beit Midrash, Colorado, 2012).

Nee, Watchman, *Song of Songs*, (CLC Publications, Penn. 2009).

Packer, J.I., Merrill Tenney, William White, *Nelson's Illustrated Encyclopedia of Bible Facts*, (Thomas Nelson Publishers, Nashville, 1995).

Russell, A.J., *God Calling*, (Barbour and Co., New Jersey, 1985).

Stern, David, *Complete Jewish Bible*, (Jewish New Testament Publications, Inc., Maryland, 1998).

Wootten, Batya Ruth, Redeemed Israel, (Keys of David Publishing, Florida, 2006).

Vallotton, Kris, *Developing a Supernatural Lifestyle*, (Destiny Image, PA., 2007).

Zucker, David J., *The Torah*, (Paulist Press, New Jersey, 2005).

About the author

Bishop Audrey Drummonds is the founder and director of Interior Coverings Ministry and Outreach Missions in Groveland, Florida, since 2002. She has a PhD in religious philosophy and master's of divinity from Tabernacle Bible College and Seminary, with a bachelor's from Liberty University. She is the presiding bishop of the World Communion of Christian Celtic Convergence Churches into the USA. Ministry has taken her into over forty countries, including, Israel, Greece, Turkey, Peru, India, Kenya, Philippines, India, Canada, England, Mexico, Honduras, and Russia. She writes, lectures, teaches, and speaks for Interior Coverings Ministry and the WCCC. She resides with her husband in Florida.

Printed in the United States
by Baker & Taylor Publisher Services